THE
MOUNTAIN GORILLA

Boyd Norton
Foreword by Betty White

VOYAGEUR PRESS

*To Jean Anne and Scott with hopes that there will
always be mountain gorillas for you and your children and theirs*

Printed in Hong Kong
90 91 92 93 94 5 4 3 2 1

Library of Congress Cataloging-in-Publication Data

Norton, Boyd.
  The mountain gorilla / Boyd Norton.
    p.   cm.
  Includes bibliographical references
  ISBN 0–89658–134–9
  1. Gorilla. I. Title.
  QL737.P96N67 1990   90–12507
  599.88'46 – dc20   CIP

Published by Voyageur Press, Inc.
P.O. Box 338
123 North Second Street
Stillwater, MN 55082 U.S.A.
In Minn 612-430-2210
Toll-free 800-888-9653

Distributed in Canada by Whitecap Books
Vancouver/Toronto

Voyageur Press books are also available at discounts for quantities for educational, fundraising, premium, or sales-promotion use. For details contact the marketing manager. Please write or call for our free catalog of natural history publications.

CONTENTS

ACKNOWLEDGMENTS

I'm indebted to a number of people whose help made this book possible. A special thanks to Wayne and Ginny King. Having been there and having seen for themselves these magnificent animals, they provided funding to make possible further research and photography on my part.

The Professional Photography Division of Eastman Kodak made a generous donation of the only film I would consider using for a project of this importance. I'm appreciative of the efforts of Patrick Siewert in this regard.

Claude Ramsey, former Executive Director of the Digit Fund, provided assistance in my research. So too did Craig Sholley of the Mountain Gorilla Project and Diana McMeekin of the African Wildlife Foundation in Washington. I thank them all for taking time from very busy schedules to answer my seemingly endless flow of questions. Craig, especially, was helpful and cordial when I popped in on him at Kinigi while he was preparing for the all-important gorilla census in September of 1989.

I was relieved of the burden of certain travel arrangements through the help of Dave Blanton, president of Voyagers International in Ithaca, New York. As usual, Voyagers's trip arrangements were flawless. Don and Steven Turner of East Africa Ornithological Safaris in Nairobi also gave me great help with my visits to Rwanda.

At Rwanda Travel Service in Kigali, thanks to Dorothee and Charlotte and my excellent driver-guides, Calixte, Victor, and Francois.

Parc National des Volcans has some very dedicated ranger-guides; I'm appreciative of the help given by Sylvestre, Joseph, John, Mathias, and Francois.

At Voyageur Press Helene Jones had infinite patience while I fussed with changes in the manuscript as deadline was upon us. Thanks. Thanks are also in order to Bob DuBois and Tom Lebovsky for seeing the importance of this book and for making it possible.

Though I never had the good fortune to meet either one, I'm especially thankful to George Schaller and Dian Fossey. Without their dedication and hard work, it's almost certain that there would be no more mountain gorillas to write about and photograph and love.

The mountain gorilla, Gorilla gorilla beringei, *is distinctly classified from the western lowland gorilla,* Gorilla gorilla gorilla, *and the eastern lowland gorilla,* Gorilla gorilla graueri.

FOREWORD

My interest in gorillas began well over half a century ago, when I fell in love with two baby lowland gorillas, Ngagi and Mbongo, on exhibit at the San Diego Zoo.

Martin and Osa Johnson had brought these little guys back from one of their highly publicized treks through "darkest Africa." I don't even want to speculate on how they were obtained.

They were on display in a small wire cage, with only a railing separating them from the public. People could toss in food, wrappers, whatever, totally unaware of how susceptible these wondrous creatures are to human diseases. My mom and I would sit on a bench in front of their cage and watch them by the hour. I'd watch their eyes, which always seemed focused on something so far away, and oh, how I would wonder what they were *thinking*. Even as a child I could *feel* them thinking. This book's author knows that feeling.

It wasn't very long before we went back one day and found them gone. Forever.

Today, worldwide public fascination with gorillas continues to grow as we learn more about them, and fact is separated from fiction. There is also, at long last, a burgeoning if belated concern for their survival. High time. We owe an inestimable debt to those intrepid few who did so much more than sit and watch—to George Schaller, then to Dian Fossey, and to Dr. Louis Leakey for his help on so many fronts.

In June, 1985, I had the privilege of meeting Dian Fossey when she attended a symposium sponsored by the Morris Animal Foundation on "Breeding of the Great Apes in Captivity." I shall never forget her intensity and single-minded dedication to the future of her beloved mountain gorillas. Six months later Dian was murdered.

Her work, however, continues through the Digit Fund of Englewood, Colorado, now affiliated with Morris Animal Foundation, and the progress would please her, I think. At her Karisoke Research Center meaningful scientific studies continue. New dormitories have been built to accommodate visiting scientists, as well as for trackers and guides, and Dian's cabin has been rebuilt. Antipoaching patrols of four men each are sent out, at least two patrols a day. The men live at Karisoke, working from daylight to dark, seven days a week. After two weeks, another crew comes up for the next two weeks. They alternate in this manner all year and soon expect to increase the number of patrols. These antipoaching teams destroy an average of nine hundred traps and snares a year, with the result that Jozi, in August, 1988, was the last gorilla fatality attributed to poachers.

The total population of mountain gorillas has risen 11 percent in the past three years. A 1986 census placed the number of animals at 276; the 1989 census came in at 310. The signs are hopeful, barring any major health crisis, but vigilance must continue to prevent these magnificent creatures from disappearing. Forever.

The gorillas we see in our American zoos today are all of the lowland variety, slightly smaller, with a less luxuriant coat than their mountain relatives. An ever-increasing human population continues to reduce the gorilla's natural habitat and decimate its numbers, placing it high on the Endangered Species list. Laws have finally been established forbidding the taking of any more of these animals from the wild, so captive breeding is the only viable alternative.

The first baby gorilla ever born in captivity was delivered at the Columbus Zoo in Ohio in 1957. Assisting at that momentous event was Dr. Warren Thomas, now the director of the Los Angeles Zoo. Captive-born gorillas often don't reproduce, and even when they did, the attrition rate of newborns was in excess of the survival rate. So the gorillas' long-range future looked grim.

The good news, as Dr. Thomas explained, is that this gloomy statistic has *reversed* since 1982 with the advent of the Species Survival Program. The SSP has accomplished this by standardizing husbandry, enabling zoos to get in step with each other rather than using a variety of individual efforts; by medical attention standards; by sharing information; and by enlightened management.

The mountain gorilla you will not see in any zoo—only in the wild. Through the hard work and dedication of Karisoke's staff, the outlook for long-term survival is encouraging. The mystique that attracts so many to this incredible animal has struck an uneasy balance, which may buy him time in the protection of this small patch on the planet. At least for as long as it proves profitable. It could also, at any time, prove to be his undoing.

While you are enjoying the pictures, I urge you to read the text of this beautiful book. You will feel you have actually experienced this disappearing wonderland. Perhaps you will understand why saving a species—any species—has a bearing on saving your own.

—Betty White

MYTH AND LEGEND

On the very first trip I made to the forest of the Virungas I had this strange feeling that I had been here before. Mentally I was transporting myself back to childhood, vividly recalling those hot summer days spent in a southern New England forest where I played explorer in darkest Africa. The forests were not the same, of course. But there was this *deja vu*, reliving some dreams and aspirations of youth.

I remember how carefree a time that had been, the time we all savor, free from confining walls of school and happily oblivious to the passage of days. Saturday afternoon movie matinees provided fuel for a week's worth of play and pretend in the jungle-woodlots near home. *Tarzan* movies were especially popular. We all sought to emulate the adventures of Johnny Weissmuller, swinging on ropes tied to sturdy branches of oaks or maples (there didn't seem to be any of those convenient vines that Tarzan had in *his* jungle). I often wondered how he ran around in those jungles wearing next to nothing, remaining unscarred from branches and thorns and un-bitten from the many bugs that I knew must live in those jungles. After a few painful attempts at imitating Tarzan's costume, I kept myself adequately clothed.

On those humid, sun-drenched days, I would inch along on my belly through a thick duff of leaves and clawing branches for a shot at the elu-sive leopard. Of course, it was a *bad* leopard, one that had been raiding native villages and preying on cattle. Usually a battle ensued and I found myself rolling around in bush and bramble locked in a mortal combat with the wounded an-imal, armed with only a knife. Like Tarzan, I sur-vived those battles, though many shirts and pants were ripped and torn by the savage claws of the big cats. At the end of the day I returned home dirty and tired and scratched, but victorious over the marauding carnivores.

Shared by those of us who played these games day after day was common knowledge that, of all the fearsome animals of our make-believe Africa, it was the gorilla that was the most dangerous. We knew that the great apes invaded villages to carry away women and children.

I don't remember now how we arrived at that conclusion. It may have been some *Tarzan* epi-sode or a Martin and Osa Johnson documentary that provided the awesome evidence. I remember reading, often by flashlight under the bedcovers at night, numerous accounts by early explorers, adventurers whose names escape me now but whose vivid descriptions left an indelible impres-sion. Regardless of the source, it became fact in our minds: The tooth and claw made the big cats formidable adversaries, but the mighty gorilla, even when mortally wounded, could break a man's neck with one powerful blow. I survived

Ndumi, silverback of Group 11, feeding. The mountain gorilla families have been given names, such as Group 4, Group 11, Group 13, and Suza Group, to facilitate researchers' record keeping.

many an attack by lions and leopards, but the gorilla gave me the most desperate battles of my woodlot jungle.

* * *

We've all matured in our knowledge and understanding of gorillas, thanks to the efforts of such people as George Schaller and Dian Fossey. However, Schaller and Fossey began their work in relatively recent times. For most of the 140 years since gorillas were discovered by white explorers, these animals have been surrounded by myth and legend.

The very first reference to *gorilla* appears in writings from ancient Phoenicia. In 470 B.C. an expedition from the famed north Africa city of Carthage set out in a fleet of boats for the northwest coast of Africa, landing in the region of Sierra Leone and Liberia. In the dense rain forests the explorers encountered apelike forest dwellers, which they called "gorillai," and captured three of them. Described by Carthaginian navigator Hanno as "wild hairy men," there's doubt that they were, in fact, gorillas. The region also has large populations of baboons and chimpanzees, and scholars today suggest it likely that skins returned to Carthage were of those species.

An animal of Portuguese West Africa called the *pongo* is probably the first reliable reference to the gorilla and was sighted by Andrew Battell, an Englishman taken captive by the Portuguese and forced to serve in their army in West Africa. According to Battell, "This pongo is in all proportions like a man; but that he is more like a giant in stature, than a man. . . . He differeth not from a man, but in his legs; for they have no calfe . . . they sleepe in trees, and build shelters for the raine." Battell's depiction remained obscure, however, having been reported in a little-known book in 1625.

It was in April of 1847 that a missionary named Dr. Thomas Savage described in a popular publication the lowland gorilla of Gabon River in West Africa. In the *Boston Journal of Natural History* he wrote, "They are exceedingly ferocious and always offensive in their habits, never

running from man as does the chimpanzee." Savage never actually *saw* a gorilla, but instead he examined several skulls and relied upon description given him by the Mpongwe, inhabitants of the region. In Savage's account he called the animal "Enge-ena," a phonetic spelling of the Mpongwe word *ngina* for gorilla. But it's interesting to note that Savage tried to dispel at least one of the myths about gorillas. He wrote, "The silly stories about their carrying off women from the native towns, and vanquishing the elephants, related by voyagers and widely copied into books, are unhesitatingly denied. . . . They probably had their origin in the marvelous accounts given by the natives, of the Enge-ena, to credulous traders." Although the missionary never saw a real gorilla, he was surprisingly accurate in his description of one of the gorillas' most notable habits, the building of night nests for sleeping: "Their dwellings, if they may be so called, are similar to those of the chimpanzee, consisting simply of a few sticks and leafy branches supported by the crotches and limbs of trees; they afford no shelter, and are occupied only at night." But Savage managed to succumb to the temptation of exaggeration when he described how the gorilla had the strength to crush the barrel of a hunter's gun with his teeth!

Perhaps the worst hyperbole came from the pen of a French-American adventurer and hunter named Paul Du Chaillu, the first white explorer to shoot a gorilla. From 1856 to 1859, Du Chaillu explored the middle and upper reaches of the Ogooue River in what is now the central portion of Gabon. With unashamed self-aggrandizement and melodramatic prose, Du Chaillu recounted his exploits in several popular books he published in the 1860s. Calling them "wild men of the woods," he wrote of his first encounter with a gorilla: "Here was I now, it seemed, on the point of meeting, face to face, that monster, of whose ferocity, strength, and cunning the natives had told me so much, and which no white man before had hunted. My heart beat till I feared its loud pulsations would alarm the gorilla." He shot the animal, which he described as "being of that hideous order, half-man, half-beast."

A home near Rutshuru, Zaire, on the way to Djomba Intrepids Camp and Virunga National Park (Parc National de Virunga).

In a children's adventure book, Du Chaillu described another gorilla hunt, on the upper reaches of the Ovenga River of central Gabon. "The gorilla looked at us for a minute or so out of his evil gray eyes, then beat his breast with his gigantic arms—and what arms he had! . . . Again the gorilla made an advance upon us. Now he was not twelve yards off. I could see plainly his ferocious face. It was distorted with rage; his huge teeth were ground against each other, so that we could hear the sound; the skin of the forehead was drawn forward and back rapidly, which made his hair move up and down, and gave a truly devilish expression to the hideous face. Once more he gave out a roar, which seemed to shake the woods like thunder; I could really feel the earth trembling under my feet. The gorilla, looking us in the eyes, and beating his breast, advanced again." And again Du Chaillu and his companions shot and killed the animal.

Literary effect notwithstanding, the accounts of Savage and Du Chaillu about the ferocity of gorillas are not without a certain amount of truth. Research in recent decades into the behavior of gorillas has shown that the dominant male silverbacks of a family will often display threateningly, with piercing screams and chest beating. Occasionally, if this behavior doesn't frighten away an intruder, the gorilla will charge. Though the startling and unnerving charges by the animal are often bluffs, few would stand calmly to see if this massive, rushing animal would stop, especially when the explorer has heard many tales from natives about the hostility of the *ngina* and of the local people killed and maimed by the beasts.

Of course, one wonders if some of these tales weren't designed especially for the timorous voyager, partly out of fun and jest, partly to make the natives seem, to foreign eyes, brave souls for living in such dangerous domain. These early explorers considered the native people to be ignorant savages, a disdainful attitude that was not unnoticed by the natives. Undoubtedly, the

Rugabo, silverback leader of a mountain gorilla family. About 310 mountain gorillas remain, all living in east central Africa, in the area of the Virunga Volcanoes in Rwanda, Zaire, and Uganda.

12

natives noted that the white explorers paid most attention and respect when exaggerated tales were related to them. And anyway, who doesn't enjoy scaring the newcomer with horror stories? Sitting around the campfire one evening with the Mbondemo people of interior Gabon, Du Chaillu listened in fearful fascination to such fables: "Finally came the story that is current among all the tribes who are acquainted with the habits of the gorilla, that this animal will hide himself in the lower branches of a tree, and there lie in wait for people who go to and fro. When one passes sufficiently near, the gorilla grasps the luckless fellow with his powerful feet, which he uses like giant's hands, and, drawing the man up into the tree, he quietly chokes him there."

Perhaps, after finishing, the Mbondemo storytellers sneaked behind a hut to giggle hysterically over the credulity of this white foreigner.

* * *

These early accounts out of West Africa described the lowland gorilla. The interior of Central Africa and especially the higher altitude rain forests, home of the mountain gorilla, were more difficult of access and were penetrated by explorers much later than the coasts. John Hanning Speke, the famous British explorer, set forth from Zanzibar in 1861 on an overland trek to search for the headwaters of the Nile. He traveled westward from the Indian Ocean coast, turning north before reaching Lake Tanganyika (which he had discovered with Sir Richard Burton in 1858). Near Lake Victoria, in the area of present-day Akagera National Park on the border of Rwanda and Tanzania, Speke noted "some bold sky-scraping cones situated in the country of Ruanda" to the west of where he stood. This terra incognita had been named *Lunae Montes*, or "Mountains of the Moon." The loftiest of the cones were called "Mfumbiro" by Speke and what he saw in the distant haze were undoubtedly the Virunga Volcanoes. He wrote, "The Mfumbiro cones in Ruanda, which I believe reach 10,000 feet, are said to be the highest of the

'Mountains of the Moon.'" Speke did not choose to visit the region, keeping to his original goal—the source of the Nile. However, in apparent reference to gorillas, he reported that natives told him "there were monsters who could not converse with men, and never showed themselves unless they saw women pass by; then, in voluptuous excitement, they squeezed them to death."

Again one wonders how such embellished tales came about. Was it an attempt to impress the foreigners? Or was it due to the forest domain of the mountain gorilla, so forbidding to natives of surrounding regions, fueling both fear and fantasy about the gloomy haunts. Surely, on the basis of current knowledge of gorilla behavior, no one ever actually observed a woman being carried off. Yet the legend persisted in both West and Central Africa.

Firsthand observation of the mountain gorilla continued to elude European explorers. When Henry Stanley caught up with David Livingstone in 1866 at Ujiji, on the northeast shore of Lake Tanganyika ("Dr. Livingstone, I presume?"), they were two hundred miles due south of the Virungas and perhaps only twenty miles from other gorilla habitat in the forested hills bordering the northwest shore of the lake. Later, both men, on separate journeys, skirted the Virungas but failed to discover the existence of these animals.

* * *

Around the turn of this century the region of eastern Congo known as Ruanda-Urundi was claimed as a part of German colonial Africa, which also included Tanganyika. To the west lay the vast colonial empire known as the Belgian Congo. The border between the two, in the region of Lake Kivu and the Virungas, was indistinct. As a part of the last-explored and least-known lands in Africa, both Belgium and Germany had but a few border posts in the area.

In order to assert its military strength and claim to these lands of Ruanda-Urundi, Captain Oscar von Beringe of the German colonial government traveled from Lake Tanganyika to the region of the Virungas in 1899. When he returned again in 1902, von Beringe made an attempt to climb Mt. Sabinio in the Virunga Volcanoes. During this effort to scale the 11,960-foot peak, he spotted a group of large black apes above the nine thousand-foot level. Von Beringe shot two of them, but managed to recover, with difficulty, the body of only one because the animals had fallen into a steep ravine. He described it as "a large, man-like ape, a male, about 1½ m. high and weighing over 200 pounds." Because gorillas had never been reported in the region, the captain speculated that the apes might be chimpanzees, but of a size previously unknown.

Von Beringe sent the skeleton to Germany, where anatomists determined that it was a gorilla, though different enough from those in West Africa to warrant a classification as a distinct subspecies. It was named *Gorilla gorilla beringei*, known today as the eastern or mountain gorilla. Though biologists and anatomists today note that the differences between the lowland and the mountain gorilla are slight, the separate classification was fortuitous and, ultimately, had a beneficial effect. When a population census of mountain gorillas later in the century indicated numbers shrinking below four hundred (as compared to several thousand for the lowland gorilla), the species became the focus of preservation efforts.

When Von Beringe's reports became known, collectors and hunters converged on this unknown region of the Congo. Many were hunters who, to satisfy their lust for shooting animals, justified their passion by providing specimens for museums that were underwriters for the costly expeditions. Others were trophy hunters offering no rationale, looking only for new species to bag and hang on their walls or to stuff and mount for perverse displays of manhood. The net result, according to biologist George Schaller, was the killing of over fifty-four gorillas from the region of the Virunga Volcanoes between 1902 and 1925. Perhaps the worst offender was Prince Wilhelm of Sweden, who slaughtered fourteen gorillas in 1921.

An adult female of Group 11 peers through foliage.

14

People from the farms that are adjacent to Parc National des Volcans (Volcanoes National Park) in Rwanda.

We now know that such slaughter had impact far beyond the body count of the animals bagged. Invariably the hunters went after the largest animals, the dominant male, the silverback leader of individual gorilla families. Loss of the silverback is traumatic for a gorilla group. The survivors, leaderless, often scatter. Alone, the animals, particularly the young, are vulnerable to predation by leopards or to other hunters. Joining another gorilla family can be stressful, creating health disorders for the animals involved. Moreover, it's now known that a silverback, after adopting a displaced female into his family, will kill any of the new female's offspring. The mortality of infants is normally very high, with only about half surviving to maturity. Infanticide contributes even more to population decline.

Females that the hunters killed sometimes had young, and without the tender care required by gorilla infants, they perished. Some of the hunters captured the young gorillas after killing the mother and attempted to crate them to zoos. But invariably the young animals died long before they were shipped — gorillas do not adapt well to captivity. Thus, the killing of one silverback often led to the deaths of several other gorillas.

At the time of this carnage, no one knew the exact population of the mountain gorillas. Estimates ranged from as few as fifty to several thousand. One noted gorilla hunter, in obvious attempt to justify his butchery, asserted that there were several thousand mountain gorillas in the vicinity of the Virunga Volcanoes. Probably the best estimation was derived from J. M. Derscheid, who spent four months in the Virungas in the early 1920s. His figures indicated a population of between 450 and 650 gorillas. The hunting, if allowed to continue unchecked, would have spelled disaster for the mountain gorilla. Fortunately there was among those scientific collectors a man who saw a need to protect the species. His name was Carl Akeley.

Akeley was a noted naturalist and a sculptor.

16

A two- to three-year-old juvenile, part of the Suza Group. Imbaraga, the silverback leader of the group, sits in the background.

An earthen-walled banda, *with a thatched roof, is a typical dwelling on the farms adjacent to Volcanoes National Park in Rwanda.*

With the combined talents of artist and scientist, he created superb museum exhibits of wildlife and habitat. On earlier trips to East Africa he collected specimens to add to the African Hall he created for the American Museum of Natural History. While in East Africa in 1910, he heard accounts of gorillas in the eastern Congo; thus, in 1921, Akeley led an expedition to the Virunga Volcanoes for the purpose of collecting gorilla specimens for the Africa Hall. During this trek he shot five gorillas, which were subsequently shipped back to the United States and mounted for the museum display. But he also shot motion pictures and made still photographs of the gorillas and their habitat. In the three months of his stay in the region, Akeley developed a deep regard and concern for the animals and the forest domain in which they lived.

The enchantment of the Virungas and the magnificence of the gorillas dwelling there had a profound impact on Akeley. He realized that any further hunting of the animals would jeopardize their existence. On his return voyage to the United States in early 1922, he began formulating plans to preserve the gorillas and their domain. Writing to an official in the Belgian Congo, he noted that the gorilla is "a wholly acceptable citizen and not the wicked villain of popular belief . . . a splendid animal in every sense, in no sense aggressive or inclined to look for trouble." Akeley made a strong case for establishing a sanctuary for gorillas in the region of the Virungas. "If this is not done very soon," he wrote, "they are in positive danger of being exterminated. I do not think it is fair to future generations to exterminate an animal of such intense human interest as the gorilla."

Akeley, through mutual friends, carried his campaign to the Belgian government, and in March 1925, King Albert of Belgium created, by royal decree, the Parc National Albert in the Kivu Province, Belgian Congo. Roughly triangular in shape, the park encompassed Mts. Karisimbi, Visoke, and Mikeno and was about sixty thousand acres in size. Established purely for scientific purposes, the hunting of any animals was strictly forbidden.

Akeley returned to the Congo in 1926 with his wife and some biologists to continue studies of the gorillas and to photograph the animals and their domain. Along their trek through Uganda, Akeley came down with a fever and became progressively weaker. On reaching the lovely meadow in the saddle terrain between Mts. Karisimbi and Mikeno, a place called Kabara, Akeley succumbed to the infection. He was buried there, the place he had called "the most beautiful spot on earth," in the middle of the park he had helped to establish.

Through the strong efforts of Akeley's widow, Mary Jobe Akeley, Parc National Albert was expanded in 1929 to a size of 500,000 acres. Planners for the expanded park decreed the same prohibition of hunting that had been established in the larger park, providing a more secure habitat for the mountain gorilla. The park also included important game areas to the north of the Virungas, most notably the Rwindi and Rutshuru plains and the Ruwenzori Mountains—the "Mountains of the Moon."

*   *   *

The establishment of a park does not automatically ensure protection of wildlife and habitat. In the area of Albert National Park local natives continued, in places, to clear forests for crop planting, and traditional hunting of game animals persisted in certain areas. For the next three decades after its expansion, the few park wardens attempted to administer the rules and regulations with varying degrees of success. Though all depredations were not halted, most activities harmful to the wildlife and the habitat were at least minimized.

Implementing scientific research, the reason the park had been established, was slow. In particular, very little investigation of the mountain gorilla was carried out. Early hunters and collectors such as Akeley had made brief observations about their gorilla encounters, but there was no precise information on feeding habits, social life, group interactions, mating, diseases, and movement within its habitat. The gorillas themselves

A farm between the town of Rutshuru, which is on the border of Zaire and Uganda, and the Djomba Intrepids Camp in Zaire.

A youngster from a farm adjacent to Parc National des Volcans (Volcanoes National Park), Rwanda.

did not seem amenable to study. They fled at the sight of intruders, and persistent approaches seemed to provoke dangerous charges by the silverbacks. Occasional fleeting glimpses were obtained by observers patient enough to sneak quietly through the dense vegetation, but often the wary gorillas detected the presence of people and ran, crashing and screaming through the forest.

It seemed futile to carry out research here. The remote locale, the rugged terrain, the dense forest, and the wariness of the animals all added up to an impossible task for scientific researchers hoping to study the mountain gorilla. Thus, important questions about gorilla behavior remained unanswered until the late 1950s when Dr. George Schaller undertook the impossible.

RESEARCH AND ENLIGHTENMENT

Sadly, the most important fact we have learned about gorillas in recent years is that if humankind wishes to share this planet with the apes in centuries to come we can never ignore their existence, falter in vigilance, or fail in total commitment; we must cherish and protect the gorillas forevermore. — George B. Schaller.

* * *

Gorillas know no political boundaries. Their survival and well-being depend entirely upon something beyond their comprehension and control — the preservation of their habitat. The artificial divisions of colonies, states, countries, or national parks are of no concern to the gorilla, who is content to roam and feed at peace in its mountain domain. Unfortunately, events taking place thousands of miles from the serene Virunga forests have had great impact on the tranquil gorillas.

For millennia, gorilla habitat had been secure by virtue of our lack of technology and by natural forces that kept the population of *Homo sapiens* in check. By the late 1800s, that began to change, as Africa was subdivided into European colonies. The twentieth century brought with it the taming and settlement of wild lands, new towns, roads, and a burgeoning population.

At the end of World War II, there was, throughout much of Africa, a strong and growing political movement toward breaking the bonds of colonialism and establishing independent nations. In Kenya, in the 1950s, Mau-Mau terrorism heightened awareness of the inevitable — independence not only in Kenya but in other African nations as well. The conference of 1958 in Accra, Ghana, proclaimed that all African nations should achieve independence by 1961.

In the early 1900s, the region of the Virunga Volcanoes was under the rule of three nations as separate territories — the Belgian Congo, German-controlled Ruanda-Urundi, and British colonial Uganda. The dividing line, an arbitrary and artificial dashed line on a map, sliced the chain of the Virunga Volcanoes across Mts. Karisimbi, Visoke, Sabinio, Gahinga, and Muhabura, politically fragmenting gorilla habitat. After World War I, Germany lost its African colonies. Ruanda-Urundi came under Belgian control. (Later, in 1946, it was made a United Nations Trust Territory independent of Belgium.)

The Congo, third largest political entity in Africa, underwent enormous political turmoil in the period of mid-1950s through the mid-1960s. Almost immediately after achieving independence in 1960, the newly formed government broke down and factions asked for aid from the United Nations to maintain order. The very size of the country — larger than the portion of the United States east of the Mississippi River — made unification of differing tribal and political interests difficult. The easternmost Kivu Province, which contains the Virungas, was largely

Ndumi, silverback leader of Group 11. George Schaller spent twenty months in the Virungas, furnishing the bulk of information about mountain gorillas. Even the research by Dian Fossey and others who followed merely added to the basic core of information compiled by Schaller.

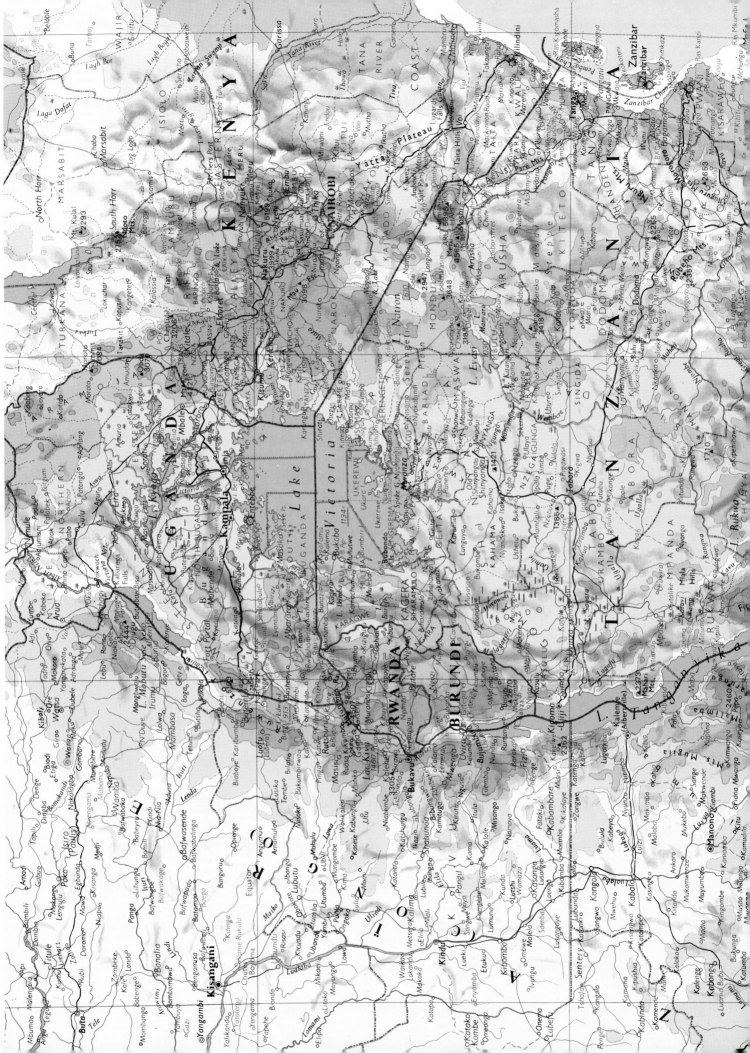

Rugabo grooming one of his females. Grooming is an important part of gorilla socializing. Most often, however, it is the silverback who is groomed by his family members.

isolated from the western portion of the Congo by poor communication and transportation. Thus, implementing any political policies of the new country was slow, and local officials often acted independently and capriciously.

Of particular impact on the gorillas was the administration — or, at times, lack of it — of Albert National Park, the very sanctuary established to protect the animals. When Ruanda-Urundi voted for independence in 1961, it became two separate countries, Rwanda and Burundi. The park was thus shared by the Congo and Rwanda. The western, or Congo, portion was renamed Parc National de Virunga (Virunga National Park) and on the Rwandan side it became Parc National des Volcans (Volcanoes National Park).

Upon independence, Belgian park administrators were replaced with locals. Few administrative directives were given, however, and there was no clear-cut government policy regarding management of the park. With an indifferent government attitude on enforcing park rules, natives of adjoining regions began to resume traditional activities of hunting, cattle grazing in the forest, and cutting the forest itself to clear land for agriculture. It seemed likely that, in time, the very boundaries of the park would be whittled away and the gorilla habitat replaced by the inevitable *shambas* to raise crops for a rapidly growing population.

* * *

In 1957 George Schaller was a graduate student at the University of Wisconsin, studying under Dr. John T. Emlen, professor of zoology. A somewhat casual remark sparked an interest in the adventurous young student, beginning a process that ultimately led to funding of a project for Emlen and Schaller to study gorillas.

In early 1959 they left New York for the Congo. Emlen, as leader of the project, was to stay for only six months. Schaller and his wife Kay

Mountain gorillas live in east central Africa in the Virunga Volcanoes, which lie along the Rwanda, Zaire, and Uganda borders. Map from Philip's Great World Atlas, *courtesy George Philip Ltd., London, England.*

A two- to three-year-old juvenile from the Suza Group finds shelter amid vines and undergrowth beneath a large Hagenia *tree during a rainstorm.*

Ndumi, silverback of Group 11. When he was younger, Ndumi tangled with a poacher's snare and lost his right hand. Snares and traps, used to kill small game for food, are still a threat to gorillas–particularly young ones.

planned to remain for another eighteen months to complete the study.

The chosen study site was located in the ten thousand-foot saddle between Mts. Mikeno and Karisimbi and was called Kabara ("Place of Rest" in Swahili). It was the same meadow where Carl Akeley had been buried thirty-three years earlier. The arrival of Emlen and Schaller seemed a fulfillment of Akeley's original dream to study the mountain gorillas, but one that remained uncompleted after his untimely death.

Nearly all previous expeditions to the Virunga domain had assumed the gorilla to be dangerous enough to warrant firearms for protection. The threatening and frightening chest-beating displays seemed to justify such measures, and there were many reports of gorillas charging people, though little actual evidence that humans had been injured (the animal was usually shot). Even Akeley warned in his writings that "the white man who will allow a gorilla to get within ten feet of him without shooting is a plain darn fool."

As a student of animal behavior, Schaller believed that few animals represent a real threat and that many, as his experiences with Alaska grizzly bears seemed to confirm, often display or charge as a bluff. So he embarked on his study without the protection of a weapon, relying on a hunch that gorillas are basically shy animals and not as aggressive as previous literature indicated. In addition, he theorized that many animals can detect and accurately interpret certain gestures and behavior. He wrote, "I believe that even the possession of a firearm is sufficient to imbue one's behavior with a certain unconscious aggressiveness, a feeling of being superior, which an animal can detect."

The initial contacts with gorilla families by Schaller and Emlen seemed to confirm this hypothesis. Though disturbed by their approach, the animals did not behave aggressively and, in time, came to accept their presence. For their part, both men kept their presence as nonthreatening to the gorillas as possible. Because of

The Suza Group. A juvenile huddles next to the silverback (Imbaraga) during a rainstorm.

The vine Galium *is a favorite food of gorillas and can be found in most areas of the gorillas' habitat.*

the great care exercised by Emlen and Schaller and their passive behavior, in time the gorillas tolerated closer approaches, which improved the observation opportunities.

After Emlen's departure in July 1959, the Schallers stayed on to continue the studies. The conditions were far from comfortable. They lived in a small cabin built seventeen years earlier to house a park ranger. With its rough-hewn board siding and metal roof, the cabin offered scant protection from cold weather and rainy periods. Kabara's elevation, at ten thousand feet above sea level, creates a cold climate; it's common to find frost on the ground in the mornings, and the summits of Karisimbi and Mikeno sometimes receive a coating of snow. To lengthen his observation periods, Schaller occasionally took a sleeping bag into the forest with him and slept near the gorilla families at night. This gave him opportunities to study the animals as they prepared their night nests and as they awakened and began feeding in the morning.

In the study of animal behavior, great care must be exercised *not* to influence the animals by the presence of the researcher. It's a difficult task, for most animals react to the presence of humans by flight, defensive posturing or aggressiveness or, at the very least, nervousness that causes behavior modification. With time and care, the researcher can habituate some animals to his or her presence, placating the animals sufficiently to allow them to continue with normal day-to-day activity.

Schaller's sensitivity and care created an atmosphere of trust in his study animals and thus he was able to make observations on gorilla behavior and environment that not only had never been done before, but also that some researchers had predicted would be impossible to achieve. Instead of ferocious, dangerous beasts, Schaller found the gorillas to be relatively placid, peaceful animals. His presence, at first, created excitement, and the silverback leader of a group often screamed a warning and gave chest-beating dis-

Imbaraga, silverback of the Suza Group, rubs his eyes in a seemingly humanlike gesture.

Mrithi, silverback of Group 13, drinks from a small pool of water.

plays. Instead of fleeing, in time the families resumed their feeding activity, though keeping a wary eye on this intruder in their domain. When the family decided to move on, Schaller made it a point never to follow for fear that this might increase stress and be interpreted by the animals as aggressiveness on his part.

During the research period, ten separate family groups were studied in the Kabara area, these representing about two hundred gorillas in total. Schaller estimated that between four hundred and five hundred mountain gorillas inhabited the Virunga Volcanoes at that time. He made important observations on the forest zones used by the gorillas. He also documented weight, sizes, age and sex distributions, personality variations among individuals, and observed family size, structure, and behavior. The kinds of plants eaten by gorillas—even that they were basically vegetarians—had never before been verified by detailed observation. Schaller estimated that infant and juvenile mortality rate was between 40 and 50 percent—a number that seems surprisingly high considering the strong, protective bonding among family groups.

The information amassed in Schaller's twenty months of study provided a solid foundation of knowledge about mountain gorillas. Even the research by Dian Fossey and others who followed Schaller merely added to the basic core of information he compiled. He also sounded a warning that, though the gorillas of the Virungas were not yet faced with extinction, continued vigilance was necessary on the part of conservationists to ensure the gorillas' survival.

The end of George and Kay Schaller's study coincided with the Congo's period of political turmoil immediately following independence. In June of 1960, near the time of their departure, the Congo was declared an independent country. Almost immediately the central government broke down, with various factions scrambling for power. There was total lack of cohesiveness. Some provinces even tried to secede and establish

A silverback mountain gorilla, Rugabo, and family during their midday siesta. Virunga National Park (Parc National de Virunga) in Zaire and Volcanoes National Park (Parc National des Volcans) in Rwanda have been set aside as protected habitat for the mountain gorilla.

Park Rangers carry rifles as protection against the buffalo that roam the forests of the Virungas and, occasionally, as law enforcement against poachers.

themselves as independent countries. In July, United Nations troops arrived to maintain order and aid government factions in establishing a unified governing arrangement. Chaos prevailed, even in the remote Kivu district, as political entities vied for power, unions went on strike and Belgians fled the country.

Amid this turmoil and uncertain of the political future, the Schallers reluctantly left Kabara in early June of 1960 and drove to Kampala, capital of Uganda. Leaving Kay, Schaller returned to Rumangabo, the little town halfway between Goma and Rutshuru, to retrieve field notes and other belongings. Complete disorder, with drunken troops and rebels, was everywhere. After returning to Uganda, Schaller returned once again to the Virungas and, in early August, made one more visit to his camp at Kabara.

What he found was disheartening. Park administration had disintegrated almost entirely. Watutsi herdsmen, once kept from these mountain lands by park enforcement, were quick to seize on the chaos, and their cattle were everywhere in the park. The forest habitat was being destroyed. The new park administrator, Anicet Mburanumwe, was sympathetic to a plea sent by Schaller, and dispatched a small group of armed park rangers to chase off the Watutsi and their cattle. But by the time of Schaller's final departure in September, the situation was tenuous at best. Still under Belgian rule, the Rwandan side of the park was without any firm administrative direction. Cattle grazing and hunting and cutting of the forest threatened more and more gorilla habitat. The future of the mountain gorilla did not look good.

Schaller returned three years later, in August 1963. What he found was moderately encouraging. Under Mburanumwe, the region of the park around Kabara had been kept relatively free of destructive cattle grazing and the forest habitat seemed intact, much as he remembered it. Schaller located some of the gorilla families he had studied and noted that they still roamed over the same home ranges they had been in earlier. But the gorillas, though as abundant as ever, were more timid and many fled at his approach, leading Schaller to conclude that poachers were active in the region.

Within a month of Schaller's last departure from the Virungas, Dian Fossey made her first visit. The mountain gorillas were soon to have a new defender; Fossey, in all probability, saved them from extinction.

A wildflower known in parts of Africa as red-hot poker is common at the Djomba Intrepids Camp in Zaire. In the background are Mt. Muhabura, 13,540 feet; Mt. Gahinga, 11,400 feet; and Mt. Sabinio, 11,960 feet.

DIAN FOSSEY

Dian Fossey had dreamed of Africa since childhood. In the lonely days of her youth, she developed a love for animals; her constant companion was one pet or another. The passion developed into a longing to visit that continent brimming with wildlife—Africa, but it was a dream that wasn't realized for many years. After high school Dian decided on a career as a veterinarian. At eighteen she enrolled as a preveterinary medical student at the University of California at Davis, but the difficulties of chemistry and physics forced her to give it up after only two years. It was a bitter disappointment. She switched careers and, after obtaining her degree in occupational therapy, moved to Louisville, Kentucky, to work in a children's hospital.

She never gave up her dream of visiting Africa. She read all books and articles she could find, including George Schaller's newly published work, *The Year of the Gorilla*. In September 1963, after saving what money she could and borrowing heavily for the remainder, she departed for an African safari that would take her to Kenya, Tanganyika (now Tanzania), Uganda, the Congo, and Rhodesia (now Zimbabwe). It was an ambitious schedule. Despite bouts with various illnesses, her passion to experience as much of Africa as possible kept her going. Part of her schedule took her to Olduvai Gorge in northern Tanzania where she met the famed anthropologist Dr. Louis Leakey.

Though the encounter with Leakey was brief, he was charmed by this tall, intense woman. She told him of her plans to visit the Virunga Volcanoes to see mountain gorillas, adding that she planned to come and live and work in Africa someday. Though neither realized it at the moment, this conversation marked the beginning of Dian Fossey's fateful involvement with the gorillas.

Her visit to the Virungas was brief. In mid-October she and her safari guide crossed into the Congo, then began the trek up the flanks of Mt. Mikeno to a camp at Kabara. Filmmaker Alan Root and his wife Joan had been staying at Kabara for several weeks filming the gorillas. Dian accompanied the Roots on a foray into the rain forest, up some incredibly steep terrain, and she had her first encounter with gorillas—a brief glimpse of the magnificent animals through dense foliage. The confrontation left a strong impression. She recorded in her diary her absolute certainty that she would return someday to learn more about the Virunga gorillas.

Dian returned to Louisville and resumed her work as a therapist, her dreams of returning to Africa more intense than ever. By a quirk of fate, Leakey arrived in Louisville in March of 1966 on a lecture tour. She met him backstage after his talk. He remembered her and almost immediately asked her about her visit to the Virungas and the gorillas. She related her experience and repeated her desire to work in Africa, especially

Silverback Mrithi, leader of Group 13, is nearly hidden by foliage. In the background, civilization presses up against the boundaries of Parc National des Volcans (Volcanoes National Park). The only rain forest habitat left for gorillas is that which is preserved in Volcanoes National Park in Rwanda, Virunga National Park (Parc National de Virunga) in Zaire, and a small area in adjacent Uganda.

From high on the slopes of Mt. Karisimbi is a splendid view of the cultivated fields and valleys below. Rwanda is, indeed, a lovely country.

among the gorillas.

In his thirty years of paleoanthropology research at Olduvai, Leakey had acquired international fame. His reputation made it possible to secure funding grants for various projects. Six years earlier he had started one such research program on chimpanzees, conducted by Jane Goodall at Gombe Stream on the eastern shore of Lake Tanganyika. Leakey considered primate research to be of utmost importance because there was much to be learned from modern primate behavior that might aid in explaining behavior patterns of early man. Leakey offered Dian Fossey the job of studying gorillas in the Virungas and promised to secure funding for the program. She was, of course, ecstatic. Within a few months Leakey fulfilled his promise, found the research money, and instructed her to depart for Africa as soon as possible.

In mid-December of 1966, Dian Fossey departed for Africa, and in early January of 1967 she arrived in the Congo, accompanied by Alan

Root. Root had insisted on driving her to the Virungas from Nairobi because the political situation in the Kivu district was still very unsettled, and he deemed it unsafe for a woman to travel there alone. All of the eastern Congo was threatening revolt against the central government located a thousand miles to the west. The military, in particular, was behaving unpredictably in their treatment of foreigners. It seemed a dangerous time to be arriving in the region.

For two days Root assisted Dian in establishing a permanent base camp in the meadow at Kabara. The old cabin used by Schaller was a wreck, having been vandalized and partially burned. Dian's new home became a seven-by-ten-foot tent.

Dian experienced a sense of panic on Root's departure to Nairobi. She felt alone, having two local natives as camp staff, in the midst of a remote and wild region. She soon forgot her loneliness, however, and began the study in earnest. In the ensuing days she began to establish contact

Crops of wheat grow on the terraced hillsides high on the eastern flanks of Mt. Karisimbi.

with the gorillas, though the animals did not always cooperate. At one point she was charged by two gorillas, a silverback male and a large female. Forgetting Schaller's advice about not running, she and her guide retreated and only at the last moment avoided the onrushing animals by diving off the trail into some thickets.

Except for this incident, she used Schaller's method of making herself seen by the gorillas as she approached a group. In time, they began to tolerate her presence and allowed her to remain nearby and observe their behavior. Also at this time, Dian began experimenting with her own method of habituating the gorillas to her proximity. At first she mimicked the *pok-pok-pok* sound of chest beating, but soon realized that this was conveying the wrong information to the animals. Gorillas use the chest-beating display as a signal or warning. It's indicative of a state of excitement or alarm.

Gorillas have various vocalizations, each carrying some message to others. Among these is a deep *mahemm* sound, somewhat like a musical clearing of the throat. It appears to convey a signal of reassurance — that all is well — and contentment. By imitating this, and pretending to feed on the same plants as the gorillas, Dian was able to gain the acceptance of the animals and to eventually work in even closer proximity than Schaller had.

Dian also discovered that the gorillas and their habitat were not as well protected as they might have been. She stumbled upon alarming evidence of poaching activities within the park boundaries. The Batwa people, a pygmoid tribe of forest dwellers, hunted duiker antelope, bushbuck, and bongo by using snares or spears or bows and arrows. Dian and her assistants even found confirmation that gorillas were killed on occasion and the heads and hands of the apes sold as grisly souvenirs.

The national park administrator, Anicet Mburanumwe, seemed powerless to control this incursion of park land. The too few rangers on

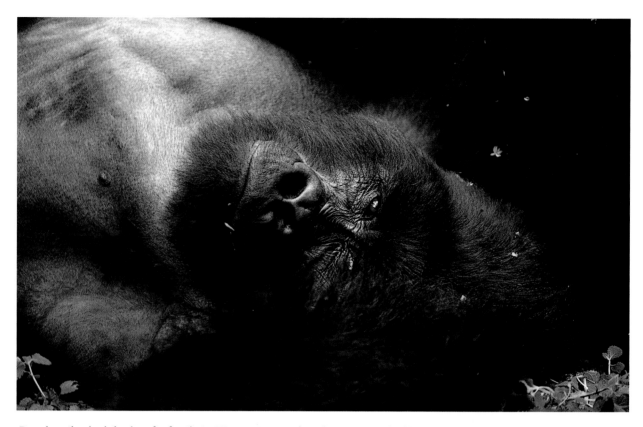

Rugabo, silverback leader of a family in Virunga National Park in Zaire. I had heard that Rugabo had a reputation of being unfriendly, but he could not have been more cordial during my visit. Those eyes. . . . I wondered what he was thinking of us.

patrol were so underpaid that they readily accepted bribes of fresh meat from the Batwa in return for looking the other way. Moreover, the unsettled political situation was of more concern to the central government than administrative policies of a national park. For Dian it was the beginning of many years of frustration in dealing with poachers in the domain of the gorillas.

Dian's studies at Kabara came to an abrupt halt in July of 1967, scarcely six months after beginning. She returned to camp one day to discover soldiers with orders from the park director, Mburanumwe, to evacuate her from Kabara. She was furious, but the order had been issued to protect her. Unbeknownst to her, the eastern Congo, including the Kivu Province, was under a state of siege. European mercenaries had joined with a rebel leader to take over this region of the Congo. Anti-white sentiment among loyal government troops had reached a dangerous level, and there were rumors of atrocities being committed on both sides.

It was a harrowing three-week period in which she first escaped to safety in Kisoro, across the border in Uganda, then attempted to return to Kabara. She was detained in Rumangabo. Once more she made her way back to Kisoro, under menacing and possibly life-threatening circumstances. She remained in Kisoro, frightened, frustrated, and angry over losing her chance to study her beloved gorillas.

Kisoro is a little town lying on the main route that crosses Uganda to the Kivu region of the Congo. It also lies near the main route into Rwanda. Several years earlier Walter Baumgartel had built the Traveler's Rest Hotel in Kisoro, a haven for travelers and, he had hoped, something of a tourist center. Well before Dian Fossey's arrival, Baumgartel's benevolent feeling toward the nearby mountain gorillas had prompted him to write to Louis Leakey in hopes of convincing him to establish a research program on the animals as he had with chimpanzees. Baumgartel had met Dian Fossey on her first visit in 1963 and

Mrithi, silverback of Group 13, sits by himself in a small grove of bamboo, feeding quietly and, seemingly, contemplating.

on her subsequent return six months earlier with Alan Root. He was a welcome solace to her and he urged her to remain with him at Kisoro until some measure of political stability was reestablished in the Congo.

News of Dian's predicament spread. Within days the U.S. ambassador to Rwanda came to Kisoro and, at his urging, she returned with him to Kigali, Rwanda's capital.

* * *

Dian Fossey's dream seemed to come to an end before it began. The violent political situation in the Congo made it far too dangerous for her to return. Furthermore, no one could say for certain when, or if, any stability might be reestablished in the region. It could be months, maybe years, before the situation stabilized and it became safe for people to travel there once again.

In early August, Dian's fortune changed again when she met Rosamond Carr at a party given by the American Embassy in Kigali. Owner of a small plantation near Gisenyi, near the base of Mt. Karisimbi, Carr raised flowers commercially to sell to hotels and vendors throughout the country. An instant rapport united the two, and they were to become lifelong friends. Shortly after their first meeting, Carr introduced Dian to Alyette de Munck, a recent Belgian émigré from the Congo who owned an adjacent plantation to Carr's. Sympathetic to her plight, de Munck invited Dian to stay with her and to use her home as a base for exploring the nearby Virungas from the Rwandan side.

At first, Dian had little enthusiasm for transferring her study area to the Rwandan side of the Virungas. It had been rumored that, through years of neglect and corruption by officials of Volcanoes National Park (Rwanda's portion of the original Albert National Park), gorilla habitat had been destroyed and both poaching and illegal cattle grazing were rampant. But local inquiry indicated that occasionally gorillas were sighted in the forests in the vicinity of Mts. Karisimbi and Visoke.

Dian began making forays into the forested slopes of Mt. Karisimbi, looking for signs of gorillas and for a possible new locale for a study area. For ten days in early September she trekked through the forest, making contact with one group of gorillas on the north slope of Karisimbi near the Congo border. For the most part, however, she was dismayed. Her suspicions and the rumors were confirmed: Everywhere there were signs of poaching and incursions of cattle. For decades the Parc National des Volcans had languished in neglect because of a lack of enforcement of park rules. Batwa roamed at will, boldly hunting and setting snares and traps for game such as duiker and bushbuck and buffalo. For years park rangers had accepted bribes of fresh meat in return for ignoring the illegal activities. Tutsi cattle by the hundreds destroyed prime gorilla habitat.

Even worse, about ten thousand hectares of land, about one-third of the park's original area, had been excised as a scheme for growing pyrethrum, a natural insecticide and a cash crop for export. Prime gorilla habitat consisting of bamboo and *Hagenia* forests were being cut and burned on the eastern slopes of Karisimbi preparatory to planting pyrethrum. (The project turned out to be a financial bust when, later, the pyrethrum market dropped precipitously. By that time the damage had been done, however, and gorilla habitat was irretrievably lost.)

During her exploratory forays, Dian spotted, from high on the slopes of Karisimbi, possible gorilla habitat in a broad, relatively flat saddle between Mts. Karisimbi and Visoke. On September 24, 1967, accompanied by de Munck, she trekked into this heavily forested area and set up a camp. She called it Karisoke—derived from the names Karisimbi and Visoke—and for the next eighteen years she spent her life studying her beloved gorillas in this lovely spot.

* * *

In retrospect, the events leading to Dian's abrupt departure from the Congo and to the establishment of the Karisoke Research Center in Rwanda were fortuitous, both for Dian and for

Confiscated snares. These devices are used by poachers to capture game such as duiker, bushbuck, and sometimes even buffalo for meat. Unfortunately, gorillas sometimes get caught in snares and resultant wounds can cause infection and death or loss of limbs.

the gorillas. This Rwanda-based camp provided a relatively stable situation that might not have been certain had she remained in the Congo (later to become Zaire). In the ensuing years the politics of Zaire remained more volatile and uncertain than those of Rwanda. Furthermore, in the tiny country of Rwanda, the central government was closer and more accessible from her research center than in Zaire, Africa's third largest country, where the capital was a thousand miles away: Many times Dian needed help from the government to control poaching.

Defying rumors that few gorillas remained on the Rwandan side of the Virungas, almost immediately Dian made contact with three different families. The first of these she named Group 4; it was actually a group of Batwa poachers who led her to the family the first time. Perhaps because this was her initial family contact in Rwanda, Group 4 was to become Dian's favorite and the subject of her most intensive studies. The group was led by an old silverback that Dian named

Whinny because of his high-pitched, horselike whinnying sound that he made as a warning. Uncle Bert was a younger silverback in the clan. A young blackback male, estimated to be about five years old, she named Digit because of a crooked finger. Digit was to become the favorite — and most famous — of all her study animals.

Dian had chosen well the location of her research center. The region around Karisoke contains some of the loveliest of Virunga rain forest. The most common tree here is the *Hagenia abyssinica;* the trees' trunks occasionally grow to eight feet in diameter. With broad, spreading limbs and a furlike covering of mosses, lichens, and ferns, *Hagenia* trees are reminiscent of something out of a J. R. R. Tolkien story. One expects to see Hobbits appear from behind a massive *Hagenia.* The tall, slender *Hypericum lanceolatum* is also abundant in the area. At certain times of year, the bright yellow flowers of *Hypericum* glow against the green foliage. The tree is host to a parasitic plant much favored as food by the gorillas, and

Rangers in Parc National des Volcans (Volcanoes National Park) maintain radio contact with park headquarters in case of emergencies or signs of poaching activities.

The boundary of Volcanoes National Park in Rwanda is a distinctive tract of land: On one side it is wilderness forest; on the other, cultivated croplands.

the thin, springy branches of *Hypericum* are often used by gorillas for building their night nests. The buds of a third tree, *Vernonia adolfi-friderici*, are eaten by gorillas, and the wood itself is sometimes eaten.

Vegetative zones vary greatly in the Virungas. Some areas are covered by thick bamboo forest, gloomy places where little grows except the tall, slender green stalks. In places the bamboo grows so closely together it forms an impenetrable barrier. During the months of heaviest rain, October through December, gorilla families will migrate to these forests to feed on fresh green bamboo shoots.

In places the *Hagenia-Hypericum-Vernonia* forest is dense with undergrowth and the vegetation is so thick that it becomes impossible to see more than few feet. Travel in such parts of the forest can be grueling, especially if it requires climbing up steep slopes, which is often the case. Sharp-bladed *pangas* are necessary to cut a path through the dense foliage, and progress is agonizingly slow at times.

Dian Fossey thrived in this world, one filled with lush greens of various hues and rich aromas that came from flowers and damp earth and decaying wood. Within sight of Karisoke were three of the major volcanoes. The closest, 12,172-foot Mt. Visoke, derived its name from the native word meaning "place where herds are watered." In times past, herders used Ngezi Lake on the northeast slopes of the mountain to water their cattle. Mt. Karisimbi, 14,782 feet in elevation, often had a cap of snow or hail, prompting its name, a derivation from *nsimbi* meaning "white cowry shells." The rugged and barren upper slopes of 14,553-foot Mt. Mikeno gave rise to its name, which means "poor," apparently in reference to it being a poor place to live.

A short walk from camp brought into view the other Virunga Volcanoes: 13,540-foot Mt. Muhavura's (also called Muhabura) name means "he who guides the way"; Mt. Gahinga, 11,400 feet, whose name translates to "hill of cultivation" (apparently Rwandan farmers traversed its slopes on their way to Uganda to obtain hoes for their gardens); and finally, 11,960-foot Mt. Sabinio ("father of teeth"), with its five jagged and serrated summits.

For the next eighteen years Dian Fossey never grew tired of the sights, sounds, and smells of this magnificent place. It was her world. And the gorillas became her family.

* * *

At the end of her first year at Karisoke, Dian had spent many hours observing four gorilla groups: 4, 5, 8, and 9. In addition, five other families were found and she was able to identify a total of eighty individual gorillas, a number that represented about one-quarter of the estimated remaining mountain gorillas at that time.

Her major problem, one that plagued her for many years, was poaching and cattle grazing. Traps and snares posed great risk of injury to her gorillas. Prime gorilla habitat was being destroyed by cattle grazing in the forest. From the start she confronted Batwa hunters and warned them that they were to cease their activities. Likewise with Tutsi herders. But both the Tutsi and the Batwa refused to take her seriously. Only after she began a regular routine of destroying snares and traps and driving cattle out of the forests did the Batwa and Tutsi realize that their transgressions would no longer be tolerated. Dian led regular patrols and, in addition to demolishing snares and traps, she burned the *ikiboogas*, small temporary shelters used by the poachers while in the forest. Her actions soon gained her a reputation as being *kali*, Swahili for "fierce."

Her ferocity, she felt, was justified. There were so few mountain gorillas left that everything had to be done to protect them. In later years, Dian often found herself at odds with other researchers who came to Karisoke because they did not share her obsession with antipoaching activities. To her it was part of the job.

On a typical morning, Dian arose at 5:30, had her tea, slipped on a rucksack with her notebooks and camera, and set off with one or more of her native trackers and guides as early morning light

began to filter into the dense forest. Often it was possible to locate a particular gorilla family easily because they didn't move far from the previous day's locale. After finding the group's night nests, the gorillas were tracked a short distance to where they were feeding. At times, however, a family might move a considerable distance because of interaction with another group. Then, skillful tracking techniques were required to find the gorillas' new locale—techniques she soon acquired.

The remainder of the day was spent in close proximity to the gorilla family, and their lives became her life. She made notes of food and feeding patterns, interaction of individuals, vocalizations, movements—anything that could give a complete picture of gorilla life and behavior. She watched as members of families—particularly Group 4—grew from infancy to adulthood. She mourned the death of patriarchs and matriarches and infants. She watched as leadership, through death, was passed on to another silverback or a younger blackback. She paid special attention to illnesses and injuries. (As a scientist, however, she let nature take its course and did not try to treat injured or sick animals.) She also observed the sometimes violent interactions between different families, interactions that occasionally resulted in death or serious injury to some of the gorillas. At the same time, she noted benign and benevolent behavior between other, separate families and puzzled over these disparate patterns of behavior.

While Group 4 was undoubtedly her favorite, Dian divided her time among other families and developed a great rapport with the animals. Group 5 was led by a magnificent old silverback she named Beethoven and a second, younger silverback she named Bartok. Group 9 was a "ghost group," discovered a few months after establishment of Karisoke. Led by the silverback Geronimo, Group 9 was a considerable distance from camp, roaming over an area partly shared by Group 8 near the Congo border. It was in Group 9 that Dian first observed the tragic results of poaching activity. A young adult female in the prime of life had become entangled in a trap, ren-

Cattle graze near the boundary of Parc National des Volcans (Volcanoes National Park). In past years, cattle grazing within the forest destroyed important gorilla habitat. Grazing in the park is now halted and is strictly controlled.

dering her right hand useless. Swollen and infected, the hand hung limply from the wrist. In obvious pain, the young gorilla continued to feed but after two months disappeared—apparently succumbing to the injury. This and many other instances of injuries from traps and snares strengthened Dian's resolve to eliminate poachers from the Virunga domain.

Dian discovered that Group 8 was particularly easy to habituate to her presence, because the dominant silverback had a tolerant, easygoing nature and seemed to actually enjoy her presence. She named him Rafiki, a Swahili word meaning "friend." Nearly three years later Dian recorded an extraordinary event while observing Group 8: the first friendly, physical contact between a wild gorilla and a human being. Peanuts, a young blackback male of the group, was feeding nearby and inquisitively meandered close to her. Dian first pretended to feed, then lay back on the foliage and extended her hand on the ground, palm up. Peanuts approached and extended his own hand, touching hers. Excited by his own boldness, he gave a rapid chestbeat, then nonchalantly wandered back to the group.

The extraordinary event was recorded on film by National Geographic photographer Bob Campbell. For Dian it was one of the most rewarding experiences of her years of study—to be so totally accepted by the gorillas. Later in her studies it became routine for gorillas to groom her, sit on her lap, steal her pack or her notebooks or camera. But on that day in 1970, her contact with Peanuts was a unique incident.

* * *

With publication of her National Geographic articles, Dian Fossey became a celebrity. There were lecture tours in the United States and in England. She managed to complete work on her Ph.D. thesis and was awarded her degree from the prestigious Cambridge University. But despite her travels and fame, Karisoke was her home and she longed to be there whenever she was away.

After her first few years of research, it became apparent that there was far too much work for just one person to handle. Gradually she accepted others. Over the next several years a steady stream of students and researchers passed through Karisoke. Some stayed and completed important work. For others, tenure was brief. Dian was a difficult taskmaster. She demanded complete dedication to "her" gorillas. Moreover, the Virunga forest was a difficult place to work: Treks to gorilla families often involved miles of exhausting walking up and down steep terrain, through dense undergrowth. There was little social life at Karisoke, and living conditions were spartan. Many were simply not capable of dealing with the lonely existence there. Work days began at dawn and ended, at least as far as observations were concerned, at dusk. Evenings were used to type up field notes made during the day. In addition to field observations of gorillas, Dian demanded that a certain amount of time be given to antipoaching activities. This often entailed long, strenuous treks through the dense forest to locate traps and snares or poachers' camps.

Dian's complete dedication to the gorillas created for her a lonely existence, even when other people came to work at Karisoke. In his book *Woman in the Mists*, Farley Mowat documented from Dian's personal diaries her brief and intense love affairs, with Louis Leakey, with Bob Campbell, and with a French doctor from nearby Ruhengeri. But her life centered around Karisoke and in the final analysis her complete emotional commitment was to the gorillas. She could not and would not leave her work.

Despite her notoriety, which helped to publicize the plight of mountain gorillas, there were continuing threats to the animals. Not long after establishment of Karisoke, it came to Dian's attention that the Cologne Zoo had paid Rwandan government officials and enlisted the aid of local hunters to collect two young gorillas for the zoo. Dian discovered the abducted gorillas and demanded that they be delivered to her. The animals were brought to Dian, near death. She nursed them back to health and then had to relinquish them to the government for shipment to

Cologne. They died after some time in the zoo.

* * *

Tragedy was inevitable. Natural deaths occurred from time to time and she mourned them as she would friends. However, she also used the opportunity to perform autopsies and gathered important information about diseases and parasites that affected gorillas.

Group 4, the family that received Dian's most intensive study, had fourteen members when she first began her observations. Whinny, the old silverback leader, died in May 1968 of peritonitis, pleurisy, and pneumonia. She estimated his age at fifty to fifty-five years.

Uncle Bert, the fifteen-year-old silverback, became the group's new leader. For the next several years Dian observed the lives and transitions of the various members of Group 4. The death of the old leader was traumatic and thrust responsibility on the young, inexperienced silverback. Dian noted that the dominant female, whom she had named Old Goat, played an important role in the group leadership. And during this time Digit, the young blackback, was learning the responsibilities of leadership that would someday have been his. Increasingly, he took on the task of lookout and scout, warning the group of approach by people or other, hostile gorilla families.

Even after ten years of diligent work at Karisoke attempting to halt poachers, poaching continued. On the last day of December 1977, poachers killed Dian's beloved Digit. The young, friendly gorilla had been serving as sentry and, detecting the approach of poachers' dogs, he attempted to fight off the intruders as the family fled. He was speared to death and his head and hands were cut off. Dian buried her friend near her cabin at Karisoke. So widespread was the fame of Dian and her gorillas, that the story of Digit's death was broadcast by Walter Cronkite on the CBS Evening News.

Tragedy continued to stalk Group 4. In July, Uncle Bert and a female, Macho, were killed by poachers. Macho's infant, Kweli, died later of wounds received in the raid. An enraged Fossey began a thorough investigation and learned that the director of Parc National des Volcans had received a bribe from a European zoo and, working with known poachers, ordered the capture of a young gorilla for the zoo. He further stipulated to the poachers that the gorilla be from one of Fossey's study groups (apparently as punishment for her vehement antipoaching work).

In Dian's own view, the Rwandan government actually reaped financial rewards from the gorilla deaths. Money poured in from around the world to aid in protecting the gorillas. However, instead of using the funds for more antipoaching efforts, the government bought shiny new vehicles, built fancy facilities and laid plans to build paved roads into and around the Virungas to facilitate increased tourism. Fortunately, the road-building plans never materialized, due to Dian's objections.

These events began, for Dian, a worsening relationship with corrupt officials and a battle to save the gorillas from government exploitation. Eventually some of the poachers guilty of the gorilla deaths were tried and sentenced to jail terms. The corrupt park director was never charged with a crime, however. In time he was replaced.

For Dian, spreading fame was a mixed blessing. While more funds were forthcoming for continued research and antipoaching efforts, her notoriety brought unwanted and unannounced visitors to Karisoke. Many were reporters and television people. Some were tourists attracted by Dian's own articles and news stories about her work. The Rwandan government was beginning to realize that the gorillas held great potential for a lucrative tourism industry. Each new tragedy that befell the gorillas created more publicity that attracted more tourists. Perhaps, as they became more imperiled, people began to realize that the mountain gorilla might soon become extinct. Better to visit them soon before they disappear.

Dian saw tourism as a threat to her studies. Large groups of visitors create stressful conditions for the gorillas and adversely affect their behavior. Since gorilla behavior was the prime

A young adult gorilla, part of Group 13, sits beneath a Hagenia tree.

Overleaf: Storm clouds envelop Mt. Sabinio, seen from high on the eastern slope of Mt. Karisimbi.

focus of her studies, tourism could have skewed the observations of researchers and might have caused inaccurate conclusions to be drawn.

Increasingly, the Rwandan government sought to develop a large tourist industry centered around the mountain gorillas. As one of Africa's poorest nations and with a population growth of almost 4 percent a year, Rwanda badly needed the inflow of foreign capital generated by tourists.

The conflict deepened. In the two years following the deaths of Digit and Uncle Bert and Macho and Kweli, Dian became evermore intensive in her antipoaching activities. She also frequently rebuffed the reporters and tourists sent to Karisoke by the Director of ORTPN, Rwanda's department of tourism. In retaliation for her actions, government officials began to pressure the U.S. Consulate to force Dian to leave the country.

For almost three years following the deaths of the gorillas, Dian was frustrated at every turn. Her intensified efforts at capturing and punishing poachers antagonized the government even more. Finally, in late 1979, she agreed to accept a research and teaching post at Cornell University. This academic break also would give her opportunity to finish her book, *Gorillas in the Mist.* In March of 1980 she left Karisoke, after agonizing arrangements had been made for a new director at Karisoke. (She had great misgivings about the interim director, doubts that later proved to be correct and almost disastrous for Karisoke.)

When Dian returned to Karisoke nearly three years later, she found that the director had allowed the facilities to deteriorate badly. Even worse, he had virtually halted antipoaching activities during Dian's absence, with the result that several gorillas had been killed and at least one young gorilla captured for the zoo trade. She was outraged and immediately resumed antipoaching patrols with a vengeance.

Gorillas in the Mist was published in July of 1983 and Dian's fame grew. Throughout August, September, and October she toured the United States as part of the publicity campaign for the book. In late November she returned to Karisoke, exhausted from the book promotion schedule. Dian's health, though improved during her sabbatical at Cornell, deteriorated. Undoubtedly, stress contributed to her ill health, stress created by trying to direct researchers at Karisoke, run the antipoaching efforts, raise funds and do battle with the director of ORTPN.

Though she resisted tourism, Dian was not against the idea of visitor-generated income becoming a source of revenue for the impoverished country. In fact, she saw carefully controlled tourism as a way of gaining more support to save the gorillas. The key was in controlling the impact of visitors on the animals. She insisted that her study groups *not* be used for tourist visits but that separate gorilla families away from her study area be habituated for visits.

In 1984 there was a new director of ORTPN who initially was friendly to Dian and seemed in agreement with her plans to protect the gorillas. However, his congeniality soon changed and he became increasingly hostile. Normally Dian would not have cared about how the director of tourism felt about her, but in order to renew her visa to stay in Rwanda, it was necessary to get recommendation from ORTPN. This became increasingly difficult to do, and only through great persistence was she able to get her visa extended —for a period of only six months.

In March of 1985, when it was time to renew her visa again, Dian sought the intervention of the U.S. Embassy in Kigali, since the director of tourism would not even meet with her. Once more it was for another short term of six months. The government was using the issuance of her visa to intimidate her, hoping that she would approach her antipoaching activities with less fervor and stop meddling in their plans for increasing tourism. She was not intimidated. In fact, in May her antipoaching unit captured the most notorious of the poachers, the man responsible for the deaths of Digit and Uncle Bert and the others. Apparently fearful of his life while in the hands of this fiercely dedicated woman, the man gave her an enormous amount of information regarding Rwandan officials involved in illegal activities, activities involving gorilla and ivory

Group 13: Kwishima, with her infant, Kageli, riding on her back, moves along slowly through the forest feeding.

trade.

Though she probably did not realize it at the time, this knowledge may have put her life in jeopardy.

In June, Dian left for the United States where she appeared on the "Tonight Show" with Johnny Carson. The result of this appearance made millions more people aware of the plight of the mountain gorilla and of the dedication of this woman to save them. Later, after having minor surgery for an eye condition, she once more returned to Rwanda around the middle of July.

Almost immediately she was faced with the problem of getting her visa renewed yet again. Moreover, she heard a rumor that ORTPN was planning to take control of Karisoke and run it for their own purposes. The rumor was

confirmed in a confrontation with the hostile director of tourism—ORTPN intend to give primary emphasis to tourism and research would be secondary to earning money for the government. Again Dian had to use friends in other Rwandan offices and was able to get renewal of her visa, but for only two months!

The agonizingly slow process was repeated in early October and again the visa was only for two months. Finally, in early December of 1985, after once again being refused access to the director of tourism, she approached an acquaintance in the office of Rwanda's president. To her delight, a visa was granted for two years! She was now assured the opportunity to continue her work without constant interruption and stress of obtaining a visa. She returned to Karisoke happi-

Rugabo and one of his youngsters. Maybe I'm being anthropomorphic, but this seems an image of a doting father. Besides, who are we to suggest that only humans are capable of expressing love and affection?

er than she had been for months and began making plans for the annual Karisoke Christmas celebration with her staff. More importantly, however, she was now free to continue her work with her beloved gorillas.

* * *

Dian Fossey was murdered in the early morning hours of December 27, 1985. Her assailant attacked her with a *panga*, a large machetelike knife used for cutting dense vegetation. The *panga* was her own. Fingerprints were destroyed by mishandling of the weapon after her body was found. In fact, it appeared that much important evidence was destroyed or lost by investigators.

Dian was buried at Karisoke in a grave next to the gorillas that had preceded her in death—Uncle Bert, Macho, Kweli, Nunkie, over a dozen in all, and most notably her friend Digit.

In a bumbling attempt to save face against world criticism, the Rwandan government indicted Wayne McGuire, a graduate student hired by Dian a year earlier, and Emmanuel Rwelekana, a former tracker for Dian. McGuire fled to the United States, with the aid and urging of the U.S. Embassy. He was tried, *in absentia*, and sentenced to die by firing squad, but there is no extradition treaty between the United States and Rwanda. Rwelekana, it was reported, hanged himself in prison.

Important work is being carried on today at Karisoke, the way Dian would have wanted. The camp remains an important and vital research center for the study of mountain gorillas. Poaching has diminished greatly, and in the five years since her death there has been a measurable increase in the population of mountain gorillas in the Virungas.

It's questionable whether there would be any mountain gorillas left, had it not been for Dian Fossey.

Mrithi feeding. Gorillas are vegetarians, but their food varies greatly: nettles, lobelia, bamboo shoots, wild celery, a vine called Galium, *tree bark, and sometimes certain mosses and lichens. Sometimes they will feed on grubs, snails, even dung and soil.*

FAMILY

The dawn light is softened by mist and foliage as the eastern sky begins to brighten. The air is chilled; the forest is still. Moisture from last evening's rain and morning mist has condensed and coalesced into glistening droplets on the leaves of wild celery and nettles and giant lobelia. The few sounds are muted by damp earth, soft foliage, and the pervasive mists. From a perch high in a moss-draped *Hagenia* tree, a sunbird shatters the silence with its sharp "*tssp, tssp, tssp,*" then breaks into its warbling song in a burst of notes. Then the air is silent once again.

An errant, horizontal shaft of sunlight filters through the dense foliage but is soon snuffed out by a waft of thickening mist. Mrithi, the silverback, stirs from the matted foliage of his night nest, opens his eyes, and raises his head slightly to look around. Nearby, one of the older females, Zahabu, is already sitting up and feeding on some foliage. But Mrithi decides it is too early to arise and he lays his massive head back down on his arm and dozes off.

Several other members of the family have begun to stir. Kwishima lies with her arms clutching her six-month-old youngster, Kageli, to her chest. Her immense arms almost hide the baby. She opens her eyes and looks around sleepily. Kageli, like all youngsters at this hour, is already awake and squirms to break free of his mother's arms. She keeps a firm grip to keep the baby from wandering off and getting into trouble.

Soon most of the family is awake. Leaving the nests they had built for the night, the gorillas move about slowly and begin feeding. It's a relaxed activity, for food is everywhere: leaves of the giant lobelia, the broad-leafed giant nettle, thistles, and a particularly favored vine called *Galium*.

Mrithi is awake now. Slowly, ponderously, he leaves the nest to begin feeding. The other members of the family, though they may not watch him constantly, remain aware of his presence. All activity centers around Mrithi: Where he chooses to go, others follow. When he stops, the rest stay nearby.

The sky is now bright, though the sun, after a brief appearance, remains hidden by swirling clouds. The mist is slowly dissipating. Instead of soft dreaminess, the forest is now hard-edged with reality. The angular forms of trees stand crisp and sharp in the morning light. Mrithi moves away from the night's encampment, swaying slightly from side to side as he ambles on all fours and planting the knuckles of his hands on the soft forest carpet. The others, all awake and out of their nests, follow.

Mrithi moves only twenty or thirty feet away, then stops in a dense patch of foliage. He sits. Long arms reach out to grasp some vegetation and soon both hands reach and grasp and break stalks and place the succulent food in his mouth. Wild celery is pulled up by the roots, broken, and, with teeth, the outer layer is stripped away to reveal the tender, moist, pithy interior. The

Mrithi's age is estimated to be about twenty-two years.

others have stopped nearby and feed in a similar manner. The only sounds are those of ripping and tearing of foliage and smacking of lips, followed by occasional belches of contentment. Among themselves, the gorillas converse only sporadically. As they feed amid the thick vegetation, many members of the gorilla family are hidden from the rest and it becomes necessary, from time to time, to reassure others of their presence. "*Mhemm, mhemm,*" assures all that they are nearby and not some approaching threat to the group. "*Mhaam,*" responds Mrithi in a soft, throaty growl. All is well.

For much of the morning the group roams slowly and feeds leisurely. Near midday everyone is satiated. Activity slows. Mrithi languidly reaches for a small branch, pulls it to him, then studies it for a moment before daintily plucking the leaves and placing them in his mouth. His eyes droop. Some of the others have stretched out on the ground to doze. He too succumbs and lies on his side with his arm over his head. Siesta time.

After the morning bout of feeding, the adults lie about and snooze during the middle of the day. Only the energetic youngsters are still active and this becomes a time of play. Since the feeding period often involves movement, which requires family members to stay within a reasonable distance, this midday break is a chance for the younger gorillas to burn off excess energy in play, without worrying about falling behind the moving group.

The patriarch, Mrithi, naps contentedly, but his snoozing is interrupted by Nyakarima and Kwilinda. In their spirited playfulness they have wrestled their way close to the silverback and, when one of the infants turns to run, he stumbles over the sleeping giant. Mrithi, infinitely tolerant of the youngsters, merely opens his eyes and grunts. He watches for a moment as they continue the wrestling match. Then he lays his head down again and dozes.

It is one of those rare days when the sun makes

Mrithi. An adult silverback of his size weighs about 375 to 400 pounds. With his strength and size, he'd make a great defensive lineman in the National Football League. Denver could use him. But he is serving us better by staying where he is, protecting his family and propagating the endangered species of which he is a member.

an appearance and the gorillas, like true sun worshippers, move into open areas to take advantage of the warming sunlight. Even the boisterous youngsters take time to lie in the sun for a few moments. Kwishima, especially, enjoys the sun and tries to nap as little Kageli wriggles about trying to squirm out of his mother's strong hands. On shaky legs, Kageli wobbles forward to grasp a plant a few feet away. Misjudging the distance, he stumbles forward onto the plant, causing Kwishima to open her eyes and reach out for the youngster. She picks him up and clutches the infant once more to her chest, but he wrestles free again and slides down onto the ground next to her.

The midday siesta, either with or without sun, is also a time of socializing for the animals. During the feeding periods, which often entail wandering over a wide area, there's little opportunity for the animals to mingle. Most concentrate on feeding. Now, in the warm sun, youngsters and adults alike lie close to each other, often reaching

out to stroke or to groom another's fur. Mrithi drowsily rolls over then ambles slowly to Kwishima and Kageli. With great gentleness he picks up the tiny youngster by the arm. His muscular hands nearly hide the infant. Lying on his stomach, Mrithi delicately grooms the youngster, his huge fingers picking through the fur with care and delicacy. For several moments Kageli is hidden from sight as Mrithi's great hands work through his fur. Kwishima lies on her side and watches unconcerned as the silverback meticulously parts the hairs and picks out tiny parasites or bits of dirt or bark. After several minutes he places the infant on the ground again and watches, perhaps humorously, as Kageli wobbles back to his mother.

Too often, the sunshine does not last long. Swirling clouds cover the sun and the skies begin to darken. With a few vocalizations, the group begins to move off toward an area of thicker vegetation and soon begin feeding again. Once more they range through the forest, stopping for

Mrithi, silverback leader of Group 13, takes a snooze during the family's midday resting period, and one of his youngsters plays nearby .

several minutes at a time to grasp some vegetation and stuff the delicacies into eager mouths. Kwishima feeds contentedly as little Kageli sits on her shoulders. By midafternoon the clouds have become darker. The forest now is gloomy and cold.

The first raindrops are accompanied by a crack of thunder. The explosion alarms Mrithi and, as family protector, he stands erect and screams "*Wraaagh*." The others scatter in panic, less at the thunder than the warning issued by their leader. They scan the forest anxiously for dangerous intruders. Kwishima clutches Kageli to her breast and looks over her shoulder as she scrambles into deeper forest cover.

In a few moments everyone stops and looks nervously at Mrithi, who still stands erect. Slowly, perceiving that there is no present danger, he drops to all fours and the others advance and cluster around him. The rain has now increased and heavy drops pelt the foliage and the animals. Mrithi moves slowly into thicker forest and finds a large *Hagenia* tree. He sits under the largest branches, but rain soon forms droplets on his black and silver fur. He wraps his arms about him as though he were hugging himself and looks gloomily out at the downpour. The others have scattered nearby, some seeking shelter, others merely hunkering down in wet foliage, waiting patiently for the rain to stop. Occasionally a drenched arm reaches out and plucks some foliage and stuffs it into a waiting mouth. The only sound is the infrequent smacking of lips and the constant rain pelting the foliage.

As afternoon nears evening, the rain abates somewhat and becomes a misty drizzle. The group moves about again, slowly, feeding on vegetation nearby. The ground is soggy now and each movement leaves an imprint of hand or foot in the grass and soil.

The waning light of day signals to Mrithi that it is time to begin building a nest for the night. The others follow Mrithi's lead. Carefully he picks a spot where tall, inedible plants grow thickly and, sitting amid them, bends down and breaks the stalks around him in a roughly circular pattern. Breaking leafy clusters, he stuffs these under his body then pauses to feed on a nearby edible plant. He finishes the nest leisurely, patting down more vegetation along rim. Then he feeds some more.

The rest of the group has followed the same pattern, slowly constructing sleeping nests of various sizes and shapes. As darkness sinks in, the group alternates between feeding and breaking off more material for the leafy beds. Gradually the group settles for the night, juveniles and infants sharing nests and snuggling close to mothers. Only Mrithi remains apart, some distance from the others, choosing the place for his nest where he might be awakened sooner by any intruder. He curls himself into his bed and listens for a while to the dripping of water from the trees before he closes his eyes. He sleeps lightly, for the safety of his family rests entirely on his vigilance.

* * *

For days, sometimes weeks, the general pattern of family life varies little. The group feeds leisurely from daybreak to late morning, then rests until early to middle afternoon. In recent years, however, the day-to-day routine has changed around midday, the time of the gorillas' siesta. Typically, this is when some of the gorilla groups can expect a visit from a group of strange-looking bipeds who carry objects that make clicking and whirring sounds. These creatures make unintelligible noises. But over time the gorillas have accepted these animals as being harmless, though they must be watched at all times. Fortunately, the visitors stay for only an hour or so and the rest of the day is peaceful. The remainder of the daylight hours are spent feeding until near dusk. Then, after building night nests, the family sleeps. From a human standpoint it may seem like a boring existence, but for the gorillas there appears to be total contentment with the routine. The interactions within the family are amicable, with relatively few disputes. For the most part these animals are peaceful and docile, leading lives of serenity that are the envy of human beings.

Overleaf: Rwanda.

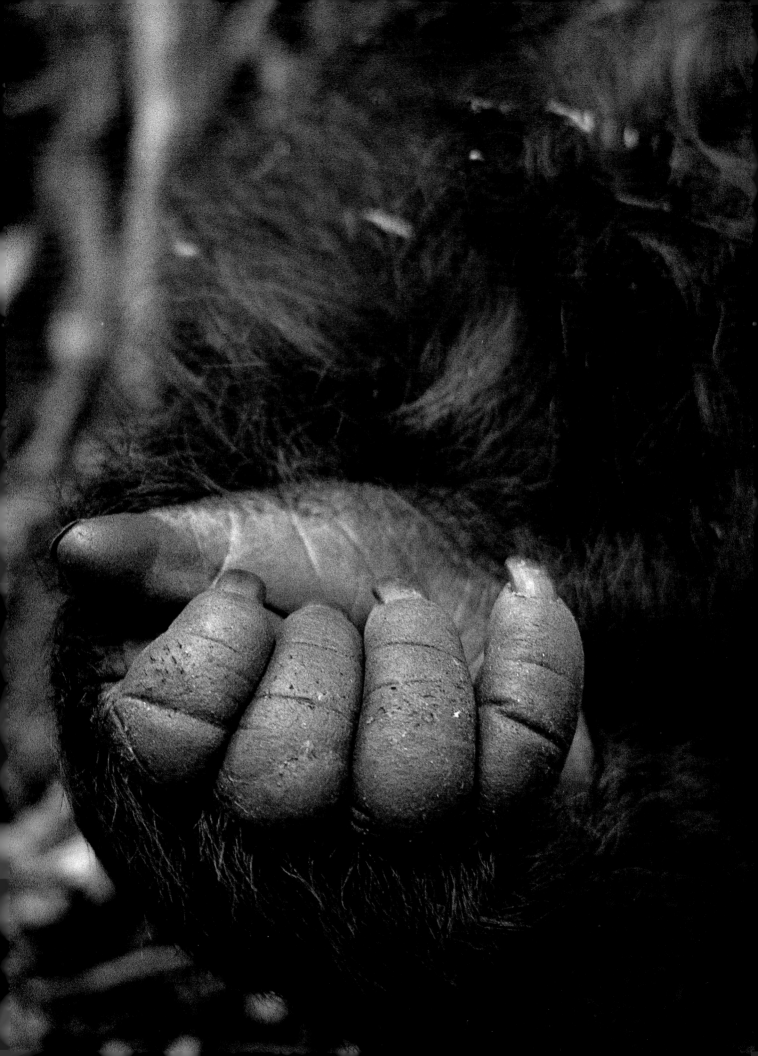

Mixed rain forest on the southwest slopes of Mt. Sabinio, home range of Group 13. The taller growth in middle is a band of bamboo forest.

Suza Group. The hand of Imbaraga, silverback of the family.

Kwishima, an adult female, and her youngster Kageli, six months old. Infants are normally carried by mothers ventrally until about four months of age. After that, the youngsters ride on mother's back or her shoulders when she is feeding.

Six-month-old Kageli and mother, Kwishima. Infant mortality among gorillas is high, as much as 40 percent. Disease accounts for most deaths; some deaths are due to interfamily fights and female transference from one group to another.

However, there are times when the peaceful routine is interrupted by interactions with other gorilla families. The home ranges of many groups overlap and, because of their aimless meandering, it is inevitable that separate families come into close proximity to one another. This often greatly agitates both sides. Each silverback frequently engages in "hootseries," a series of low-pitched *hoo-hoo-hoo* sounds, building in volume and ending with the silverback giving an impressive chest-beating display or beating the ground violently. Sometimes the displaying silverback charges through the brush, tearing handfuls of vegetation and tossing them about. These vocal and physical displays sometimes include other family members and are apparently an attempt at intimidating other gorillas. Eventually one of the silverbacks triumphs in this intimidation game and the other group leaves the area. Occasionally, however, there are violent confrontations.

As observed by Fossey and Schaller and other researchers, the dominant family's silverback reigns supreme. But his superiority is sometimes challenged, and at such times he is in danger of losing one or more of his important resources — breeding-age females of his group. The challenge comes from other silverbacks seeking to add females to their own group or, sometimes, from lone silverbacks hoping to begin their own family unit. On those occasions, the beginning hootseries become more and more furious and serious as the silverbacks engage in violent chest beating and ground thumping. Then, when one of the silverbacks feels brave enough or sure enough of his superior physical strength, he may attack the opponent in a ferocious charge. Using their large canine teeth, the huge silverbacks often inflict serious injury on opponents — sometimes resulting in death.

Overleaf: Mrithi, silverback leader of Group 13. The life span for mountain gorilla males is about thirty-five to forty-five years and about thirty-five to forty years for females.

Imbaraga, sitting Buddha-like under a Hagenia tree, waiting out a rainstorm. His stern demeanor reminded me of a calculus professor I once had, but actually, come to think of it, Imbaraga was much more tolerant and friendly.

Veterinarian Elizabeth Macfie, director of the Volcano Veterinary Center, takes notes on the health of Group 13. The center, funded by the Morris Animal Foundation, monitors the health status of mountain gorillas.

In the ensuing melee, total chaos rules in the respective groups, with other members such as younger silverbacks or blackbacks taking part in the battle. During this confusion, certain females may switch sides of their own accord, and when the battle is over they may remain with the new family. Such actions apparently keep the gene pool fresh and prevent serious inbreeding. But the violence sometimes takes its toll. Both Schaller and Fossey noted frequent evidence of injuries in gorillas. Digit, the young, subordinate silverback of Group 4, received serious bite wounds to his face and neck from an unobserved interaction with another group. It took nearly four years for the wound to heal and the infection to halt, and during that time his health was poor. During her years of examining gorilla skeletal remains, Fossey found that nearly 75 percent of the

animals had signs of healed head wounds and 80 percent had missing or broken canine teeth.

Dian Fossey first noted that infanticide was not an unusual phenomenon in gorilla families and that it often occurred when a female with an infant switched groups. The silverback of the new family killed the youngster; without the infant to nurse, hormonal changes brought the new female into her breeding cycle sooner, ensuring that there would be new offspring sired by the new silverback. Though seemingly cruel, this behavior, through millennia, has kept the gene pool of gorillas viable and insured a healthy population of animals.

For the most part, gorilla families maintain themselves in reasonable stability. Inevitably changes do occur within a family unit, changes due to deaths or aging. It's not uncommon for a

Ndumi, silverback of Group 11, and one of his females. Silverbacks will usually mate with more than one female, but a hierarchy exists with the females, as with the males, and the female at the top will be the silverback's preferred mate.

gorilla family to have more than one silverback sharing the job of protecting the group. However, even in such cases, one of the silverbacks assumes a dominant role and the other remains submissive. Usually the older male is the dominant one and the younger — perhaps an offspring of the elder — might be thought of as the heir-apparent.

Female hierarchy also exists within gorilla families. Older, dominant females often harass the females lower on the dominance scale. Also, the dominant females have closer access to the silverback, and some silverbacks show definite preference for certain females. The intergroup transference of females often provides better breeding opportunities for those females who have been in a lower social status in a particular group. In matters of social status and dominance among both females and males in a particular group, gorillas are not much different from human beings.

Newborn gorilla infants weigh about three and one-half pounds, and their body hair is sparse and lightly colored. They seem delicate, with spidery arms and legs, when compared to the immensity of adults. For the first few months of life the youngsters cling to their mother's underside whenever the mother moves with the group. Later, at about six months, the baby rides on mother's back, often sitting on her shoulders or even her head while she is feeding. Even at this age, the young gorillas seem uncoordinated and wobble about as though intoxicated. Like human infants, it takes time to develop muscular coordination.

Between one and two years of age, young

gorillas develop good coordination and often become boisterous frolickers. Adults, the silverback included, seem very tolerant of the energetic and often mischievous behavior of youngsters. Discipline is rarely physical. Instead, stern vocalizations in the form of piglike grunts or emphatic body posturing or strong looks serve to reprimand a rowdy youngster. Gorillas are tolerant and affectionate parents.

The life expectancy of gorillas in the wild is considerably shorter than that of human beings. Silverbacks may achieve the age of forty to forty-five years, females thirty-five to forty years. As one might expect from a high altitude and cold and damp habitat, respiratory diseases are common in gorillas and sometimes cause death, particularly among the older animals.

The death of the dominant silverback is traumatic for a family. If a younger, subordinate silverback has been sharing in the care and protection of the group, the transition to a new leader is somewhat easier. In some instances, however, the death of a silverback thrusts into a leadership role a younger, inexperienced male who has difficulty in maintaining family stability and protection. Sometimes, when challenged by a more mature and experienced silverback of another family, the younger leader loses not only a battle, but much of his family to the victor.

* * *

On its own, without interference from humans, the mountain gorilla has survived well through millennia. Families have formed, lived peacefully, then dissolved through natural death or group interaction.

It's likely that there have been interactions between gorillas and humans for thousands of years. Until this past century, gorilla habitat has been large enough and our population small enough to prevent serious depletion of the great apes. That's not the case any longer. The three hundred -odd remaining mountain gorillas now live in an island forest domain surrounded by a sea of humanity. The island will never grow larger, giving more room to the gorillas. But the sea continues to swell and threatens to eventually overrun the forest and the gorillas in a wave of humanity.

With care and constant stewardship, it will not happen.

Typical rain forest and gorilla habitat of the Virunga Volcanoes. The diversity of plant life is enormous. The moss- and lichen-draped trees are Hypericum.

71

DJOMBA, ZAIRE

It's funny how things work out sometimes. It was a chance remark from my friend Dave Welling that resulted in my first visit to the mountain gorillas in February of 1988. Sometime around Christmas the previous year, Dave, who had been a participant in my East Africa photo workshops, called to ask if I had ever considered making a trip to photograph the gorillas. I had to admit that I hadn't. I suppose I had thought them a bit too remote and too exotic, requiring a full-scale expedition a la Carl Akeley. Maybe not, Dave suggested. He described a newly opened camp in eastern Zaire called Djomba that he had just received information about. Why not, I replied. And so, a few months after his initial suggestion, we found ourselves winging westward from Nairobi to Goma, Zaire. Accompanying us were four others: Kathy Feng, another old friend and past workshop participant; Werner and Uta Stebner, photographers from Texas; and Sandy Watt, an investment banker from Toronto. Our destination was close to the northern border of Virunga National Park, near the little town of Rutshuru on the Zaire-Uganda border. Unlike Rwanda, the Zaire government had not, until then, promoted tourism to this region. The Djomba Camp appeared to be an attempt to develop a tourist trade, and we were among the very first to visit the camp.

* * *

Our pilot David Leonard was born in Tanzania, at a time when the area was still called Tanganyika, near the little town of Nungwe on the southern shore of Lake Victoria. I sit next to him in the Cessna 402 and over the drone of the twin engines listen to him talk about growing up in this remote region of East Africa.

Nungwe. I remember Beryl Markham's description of this gold-mining settlement: "A place of small hopes and successes, buried like the inconsequential treasure of an imaginative miser, out of bounds and out of most men's wanting—below the Mau Escarpment, below the Speke Gulf, below the unsurveyed stretches of the Western Province."

The conversation is appropriate to our locale, for we are crossing Lake Victoria north of the Speke Gulf. I'm distracted by the scene below. The waters of this, the second largest freshwater lake in the world, are dark blue in the early morning light. Fishing dhows, tiny dots on the surface, leave curving wakes that glisten like white scimitars in the sun. In my travels in East Africa, I had never before been as far west as Lake Victoria. This is new territory for me. And it's new territory in another sense, for, like our American West, explorers from other lands did not arrive until relatively recent times.

Victoria Nyanza had been discovered and named by British explorer John Hanning Speke only 130 years earlier on his expedition in search of the headwaters of the Nile. (I mentally note that, at our current cruising speed, in a matter of minutes we cover the ground that Speke took weeks to traverse.) But as recent as Speke's discovery seems on the timetable of European ex-

The market near Rumangabo, Zaire. Mt. Mikeno, 14,642 feet, is hidden by swirling clouds in background.

ploration of Africa, we are headed for a region that, only fifty years ago, few people had ever visited—the Virunga Volcanoes of eastern Zaire and adjacent Rwanda.

We had left Nairobi early to avoid the buildup of afternoon thunderstorms over the lake, but already a forbidding wall of cumulonimbus clouds looms ahead. Great white convolutions billow skyward, and graceful curtains of rain sweep earthward from the flattened bottoms of the clouds. We pick our way carefully between the clouds, aided by the green phosphorescent screen of a radar unit on the instrument panel.

We cross the Tanzania-Rwanda border, over the numerous lakes of Akagera National Park. The sky is uniformly overcast, a leaden gray. The plane drones on. Between brief rainsqualls we view the land below. West of Akagera, the hillsides are terraced to the very tops and, as we approach western Rwanda, where the land is uplifted into high peaks and carved into deep valleys, even the most precipitous mountainsides are cultivated. Despite the dark skies, the land glistens with a deep, rich verdancy.

Before descending over Lake Kivu into Goma, Zaire, I scan the horizon to the north, looking for the peaks of the Virunga Volcanoes. The mountaintops are truncated by swirling clouds and mist. Some of these peaks are higher than any we have in my home state of Colorado. They make their own weather—all of it bad, jokes our pilot. It's a sobering thought, for only a month before our visit, a planeload of American tourists, nine in all, crashed in these mist-shrouded mountains below us, killing everyone aboard.

*   *   *

From Goma on the northern shore of Lake Kivu, we drive northward, past flat-topped Nyarigongo Volcano. In 1979 Nyarigongo erupted, killing scores of people in nearby villages. The destruction is still evident in the lava flows we passed. In places the road has been rebuilt over the top of the black, cindery rock. On either side the basaltic rock is broken and jagged, the kind of lava flow geologists call *aa*, like

clinkers left over from burned coal. Banana trees sprout from the raw mass of rocks, giving an unearthly appearance to the place.

Nyarigongo and neighboring Nyamuragira are the most recent volcanoes to be formed in the Mufumbiro Range—emerging only twenty thousand years ago. Nyarigongo still has a lake of molten, bubbling lava inside its lofty summit cone. It's said that on clear nights, an eerie glow emanates from the top of the peak.

A half million years ago, this region was part of a large, flat river valley filled with thick forest. There was no Lake Kivu, nor were there any volcanic peaks. The first to emerge were Mts. Sabinio and Mikeno, spewing forth lava as they rose above the land. About 100,000 years ago, four more major volcanoes emerged: Karisimbi, Visoke, Gahinga, and Muhabura. These form the present-day Virunga Volcanoes, part of the Mufumbiro Range.

The successive lava flows, over eons, filled the valley and blocked the flow of the river northward. This mighty geologic dam created Lake Kivu; geologists claim four thousand years passed before the lake filled completely.

*   *   *

The road from Goma to Rutshuru is a well-traveled route, though in places it remains in dismal repair for vehicle passage. Villagers are moving along the thoroughfare by the thousands, most carrying loads of vegetables for market. Women are carrying staggering bundles of sticks for fuel or bulging bags of charcoal. As we drive along the curving road, past groves of banana trees and cultivated fields and coffee plantations, curious stares greet our van. When we stop near Rumangabo at a market, many youngsters surround the van trying to sell us fruit or vegetables or just to observe these strangers in their midst. Tourists, it seems, are still a curiosity here, not as common a species as in Kenya and Tanzania.

Children are everywhere, most of them wearing ragged clothes. We have a distinct impression that most of the population here is under ten years of age. The level of poverty is incredible

Nyarigongo Volcano in Zaire, seen from the highway approaching Gisenyi, Rwanda.

and, were the land not so fertile, starvation would be prevalent. Even with abundant crops, no one looks overfed; there are no fat people in this part of Zaire. An increased level of tourism could raise the living standard somewhat, but only if population growth is held in check. Ultimately, it comes down to that. Both the gorillas and the people of this region are dependent on a method of controlling a burgeoning birthrate for survival. If many more people are born into the region of eastern Zaire, even the national park may not serve to protect gorilla habitat in the desperate need to cultivate more land to feed even more people.

Continuing northward under a dark sky, I scan the hills to the east for a glimpse of Mt. Mikeno. Through mist and clouds we barely make out a massive mountain and conclude that it must be Mikeno. Not far from here is the starting point for the trek to the Kabara Meadows in the saddle between Mts. Mikeno and Karisimbi, the campsite used by Akeley and Schaller and then by Dian Fossey when she first began her gorilla studies. The steep foothills in front of Mikeno are covered with terraces, giving the appearance that the land has been covered with a blanketing patchwork quilt; every available square foot has been planted with crops.

* * *

The Djomba Camp is located near the northeast boundary of Virunga National Park, in that wedge of eastern Zaire where it adjoins Uganda and Rwanda. It is a densely populated region, though the lush vegetation masks the huts and the communities quite well.

Officially it is called the Djomba Intrepids Camp. Perched on a hilltop, the camp commands a lovely view to the north. In a wonderful bit of environmental planning, the road stops short of the camp. It's necessary to hike for about a half hour from the road end, up a steep grassy hillside, giving the camp a welcome feeling of re-

On one of the farms between Rutshuru and the Djomba Intrepids Camp, Zaire.

moteness.

Stuart Lacey greets us. Resident manager of the camp, Lacey had supervised its construction. There are three cabins, each with two double rooms, flush toilets, showers, and a central lounge or sitting room that has a fireplace. The facilities are remarkable, considering the remoteness and the difficulty of obtaining building supplies in the region. And these are probably the only flush toilets within a hundred miles.

Stuart Lacey himself is remarkable. Now in his late twenties, he had left his native England a few years earlier at the invitation from a friend living in Kenya to spend a vacation in East Africa. The friend never showed up at the Nairobi airport to meet him. So, on his own, Lacey bounced around Kenya and Tanzania for a while and, like others before him, fell in love with this part of Africa. Eventually he chucked his plans to return to England and went to work at the Mara Intrepids Camp, a tourist lodge in Kenya's Maasai Mara Game Reserve. When plans materialized for building a new tourist facility in Zaire, he was chosen to oversee the project.

Lacey speaks enthusiastically about the tourist potential of Zaire—and especially about the promise of increased tourism in Virunga National Park. Two gorilla families in this part of the park have been habituated to human visitation: the Rugabo Group and the Rugendo Group. (Adding a bit of suspense to our visit, I had heard before leaving Nairobi that Rugabo, the group's silverback, was still a bit cantankerous in the presence of humans and was prone to such occasional menacing tactics as charging people.)

Without doubt, this region is lovely and the development of a first-class tourist facility enabling people to visit these magnificent animals should be successful. Still, some malevolence seems to linger from past political turmoils, leaving me with an uncomfortable feeling. I can't pinpoint with any precision the source of my apprehension. At several crossroads, we pass soldiers carrying automatic weapons. Their stares were not friendly. The next day an incident reinforces my uneasiness: Stuart Lacey and Werner Stebner make a short trip into Rutshuru. While there they stop in a local bar to have a beer and are menaced by drunken soldiers toting AK-47s. In loud voices they proclaim that all *mzungus* (whites) should be shot. Lacey and Stebner leave the bar hastily.

Later that first evening, I watch dusk settle in the valley to the north. Smoke from countless cooking fires lies in wispy strata above the land. From below, a dim but constant sound of voices drifts up to us and, occasionally, singing. Later, after dark, one lone headlight from a car far off in Uganda stabs the velvet blackness. Otherwise, no other lights reveal that this land is inhabited.

*　*　*

Morning. Sounds of people talking and singing float up the hill from the Hutu village below. A sweet smell of woodsmoke dusts the air. We eat a hurried breakfast of scrambled eggs, anxious to push on. The sky is largely clear and the morning promises to be good by Virunga standards. To the southeast the jagged silhouette of Mt. Sabinio dominates the skyline; to its left rise the symmetrical forms of Muhabura and Gahinga, still blue in hazy early morning backlight. South of us, partly hidden by the tops of the forest canopy, are Mt. Visoke, and, with a white cap of clouds stretched over its nearly 15,000-foot summit, Mt. Karisimbi. Southwest of us is the chiseled summit of Mt. Mikeno, sharp edged against the sky.

We leave the camp shortly after 8:00 and follow a trail that takes us past cultivated hillsides, eventually bringing us to the park ranger station. There we are joined by a park ranger and a tracker. With them in the lead, we set off on the trail. The first mile of the trek is through fields that have been cleared of trees and are planted with potatoes and green beans. We are not yet in the park. However, the boundary soon comes unmistakably into view: Cleared fields abruptly end and dense forest begins.

We hike for about two hours. The trail is level for the most part, winding southwestward through the forest. It roughly parallels the park boundary for a considerable distance. The

Cultivated hillsides are precariously close to the boundary of Virunga National Park, Zaire.

A short walk from the Djomba Camp brings you to the boundary of Virunga National Park.

The Djomba Intrepids Camp, completed in early 1988.

Zairoise guides speak no English, but Sandy speaks some French and he is able to converse a bit with them. Our destination is the Rugendo family. The guides know the approximate locale of the gorillas because of their visits in the past few days. They will take us to the place where the gorillas were last seen, then begin tracking from there. They look for the night nests used by the gorillas the previous evening, knowing that the animals will be nearby.

The forest is dense and stinging nettles almost six feet tall line the trail in places. Lovely pale lavender blossoms of *Impatiens* stand out against a background of green foliage. Green. The variety of hues are almost beyond description. Lime green, emerald green, olive green, yellow-green, blue-green, pale green, dark green, even greenish black, all in a lush aggregation of grasses, mosses, ferns, lichens, narrow-leafed and broad-leafed plants, and trees. Even the stalks of bamboo are green. A green butterfly flits by. (What better disguise?)

I'm enjoying all this verdancy, thinking that, on the way back, I must stop and photograph it all, when our guides stop. Next to the trail, neatly lined up, are some slender bamboo walking sticks. They hand them out to us, one per person. Puzzled, I look ahead. The trail disappears over a precipice. So much for the easy part.

We begin the descent, slipping and sliding down the incredibly steep hillside. The trail is muddy from last evening's rain, making footing treacherous. Carrying over twenty pounds of camera equipment doesn't help things. Nor does the realization that we have to climb *up* this damned hillside on our return.

The trail is near the park boundary again. Terraced and crop-laden hillsides form one of the margins of the valley we are dropping into. A man in a field of potatoes waves at us and we return his greeting.

At the bottom, our guides suddenly leave the trail and begin hacking their way through thick vegetation with their sharp-bladed *pangas*. I'm

79

Dawn, Djomba Intrepids Camp. Mt. Muhabura, 13,540 feet (left) and Mt. Gahinga, 11,400 feet (right).

The serrated summit of Mt. Sabinio, 11,960 feet, stands boldly above the Djomba Intrepids Camp in Zaire.

The view from the Djomba Intrepids Camp in Zaire is a lovely scene of fields and forest in Uganda.

pushing and stumbling my way through vines, branches, and foliage that catch and snare camera straps and packs. Giant nettles brush against my neck and face, stinging and burning. Instead of solid ground, I'm walking over matted-down, cut vegetation. On inclines, my feet slide on the treacherous branches. After fifteen minutes of clawing and clambering through impassible undergrowth, I'm nearing the point of total exhaustion. The guide stops. Motioning us closer, he gently parts the leaves of a very thick wall of foliage and points to the dark interior. He's joking, I think to myself. I blink the sweat out of my eyes, and as they adjust to the dimness I see two eyes staring back at me! Then a shape takes form in that darkness — a head and a squat body, both coal black. A young female mountain gorilla is sitting there passively watching me as though I were the subject of her Ph.D. thesis.

This is not at all the way its supposed to happen. Where are the ear-shattering shrieks and roars and chest thumpings? Instead, the only

sounds are the raspings of six very out-of-condition people trying desperately to fill their lungs with air to keep from passing out. Our guides are breathing normally.

I stand there open-mouthed, still gasping for breath yet hardly daring to breathe. Here, almost within touching distance, is a *gorilla*. I remember Carl Akeley's admonishment about never allowing a gorilla within ten feet without shooting. I wonder if the gorillas have similar thoughts about humans.

Pictures. I grab one of the Leicas slung over my shoulder, raise it to my eye and groan quietly to myself. The light meter indicates an impossible exposure (f/2 at two days, I joke with my companions). During our trek, swirling clouds had formed, and, combined with the thick foliage of the forest, created a dismal photographic situation. And yet at the moment it doesn't matter. I simply stand and gape at this wonderful creature in front of me.

The guides move on slowly and I suddenly be-

Typical path through the rain forest of the Virungas, in this case in Virunga National Park, Zaire.

The trek to the Rugendo family took us along the edge of Parc National de Virunga, past cultivated fields that crowd the park's boundaries.

come aware of noises in the forest — cracking and snapping of branches and foliage. I look up and spot two young gorillas in a tree feeding casually. All at once the forest seems alive with gorillas. Youngsters shriek in play. A couple of adults (Male? Female? I can't tell) move slowly ahead of us, partly hidden by dense vegetation. We move among them, taking slow, reassuring steps to avoid startling any of them. Then one of the guides stops and whispers something in French. Sandy translates: Silverback. He points into an area of incredibly thick foliage and I spot this massive black and silver form moving slowly through the brush. Rugendo! He is unbelievably huge. His movement seems like a movie in slow motion, relaxed, deliberate, fluid. Walking on all four feet he pauses frequently to pick some leaves and place them in his mouth. He is obviously aware of our presence, yet he ignores us. Just as well, I think to myself; wouldn't want his full attention focused on us.

In all, we stay with the gorillas for about an hour and a half. I've shot almost a dozen rolls of film. But the light has been so bad that I don't have much hope about the publication quality of the pictures. I curse my way up that steep hillside, promising myself that tomorrow I'm gonna leave some of these lenses and cameras behind (I don't; photographers have a short recall memory for pain). We arrive back in camp by midafternoon, tired.

I kick back on the porch of the cabin and gulp down an icy cold Primus beer, reflecting on the day — a bust, photographically. Yet it's not disappointing. Simply being there in close proximity to the gorillas is an emotional high. And beside, we have another chance tomorrow with Rugabo and family.

That night a tremendous thunderstorm explodes in the skies over Uganda, but I'm so tired I sleep through most of it.

* * *

Photographing Rugabo and his family, Virunga National Park (Parc National de Virunga).

At dawn a foggy light to the northeast on the distant hills of Uganda, a pale luminescence thin and ethereal, gives a watercolor quality to the landscape. The meadow below the camp glows in pastel greens, glistening in the wetness left behind by mist and last night's rain.

Kathy has been sick all night. She is too weak to make the trip today and so, sadly, she waves us off after breakfast.

At the ranger station we are assigned two new guides and this time we follow a trail that heads straight back into the depths of the forest. I'm prepared for a trek as long and grueling as yesterday's, but after only an hour of hiking over relatively flat terrain our guides stop and lead us into the undergrowth. Once again the ranger and his tracker slice a path with their *pangas*. Judging from the size and toughness of the stems and branches they cut with ease, I conclude that they are honed to razor sharpness.

After a short distance, we break into an open area filled with chest-high plants with broad leaves. The lighting today is ideal: High, thin clouds soften the harsh sunlight yet maintain a nice level of brightness. Occasionally the sun peeks through.

Once again we hear the breaking and snapping of branches, but as yet we can't see the animals. "*Wraaagh*," shrieks a youngster. "*Wraaaagh*," answers another. To our right comes the *pok-pok-pok-pok* of chest thumping. Our guides lead us into another area of forest, though it's not as dense as yesterday's. We discover one of the night nests, an oval, dish-shaped pattern of leaves and stalks. A few feet away sits an older female; we begin photographing her. She sits quietly, tolerant of the noise of motor drives. From out of the foliage steps a youngster, perhaps a year and one-half to two years old. He joins the female, sitting next to her and watching us with mild curiosity.

Suddenly our guides make frantic gestures, motioning for us to sit or kneel down. To the left

Rugabo and family amble through the thick forest of Virunga National Park in Zaire. The gorillas spend a great amount of their time feeding or traveling and feeding.

An adult female of the Rugabo family, Virunga National Park, Zaire.

85

The silverback Rugabo grooms one of his infants in Virunga National Park, Zaire.

the foliage parts like a curtain and Rugabo emerges. Like a veteran thespian of Shakespearean theater, he struts slowly across center stage only fifteen feet from us in a lazy but deliberate four-footed, stiff-armed gait, past the female and youngster, past five crouching photographers and two guides, and, without pause, saunters slowly into another thicket. The legend of King Kong doesn't seem quite so silly.

The camera was poised, but I didn't take a single shot. I'm transfixed by a pulse-pounding, cotton-mouthed, giddy rush of adrenaline. *Jesus Christ, what a magnificent animal!* I remember to breathe again.

We follow Rugabo at a respectful distance, the guides leading. The silverback's track leads to a small opening in the forest and there he chooses to sit and feed leisurely. It's a tremendous photographic opportunity, for there is plenty of light and no foliage to contend with. Over the next twenty minutes other members of the family join Rugabo in the clearing; youngsters play and adults groom each other. The great silverback lifts a tiny baby—perhaps six months old—and proceeds to groom it tenderly. As he does so, the infant is almost hidden from view by his massive hands. Then he gently hands the baby back to the mother and rolls on his back for a nap. Occasionally, he opens his eyes to check on us and once I find him staring at me intently. Spatially, we are separated by a distance of twenty feet. But temporally how many thousands of years of evolutionary time are we apart? I wonder what thought process is going on behind those limpid brown eyes. Experts warn against making direct eye contact with silverbacks. Threat to their dominance, they suggest. Could lead to an attack. Yet I see no hint of malevolence here. I wonder if these animals are capable of understanding that there's a new relationship in effect with humans, that we occasionally visiting bipeds can now make it possible for their kind to live in relative peace, free now from most past human transgressions. Maybe, but it's still good

A young gorilla, about one year old.   *Silverback Rugabo and one of his females.*

for them to keep an eye on us. Our own track record on intraspecies behavior isn't very good.

Photographically, this has been incredible. Eastman Kodak stock has jumped several points. I joke with the others that we need water-cooled motor drives. After a while, I simply stop shooting and watch, sitting amid the litter of film cannisters and lenses and camera bodies I have spread at my knees. Too soon it's over. Rugabo awakens, stands on all fours and ambles off in a slow, deliberate gait. Just before passing from view he makes a karate swipe at a three-inch diameter bamboo. The bamboo tree, with a young gorilla in it, comes crashing to the gound. Rugabo says its time to go. We back off and leave. Go in peace, my friend. I wish you well. Thanks for letting us visit.

On the way back it starts to rain, lightly at first, then it turns into a downpour. Even with a rain poncho, I'm soaked to the skin.

But I don't care.

KINIGI, RWANDA

One of the fond memories I have from my visits to the mountain gorillas, aside from the animals themselves, is of the wonderful, melodic sing-song cries of "Bonjour, Bonjour" from the children running across potato fields to greet us as we return wearily from a visit to the gorillas.

"Bonjour," I respond, waving. They stop and wave, giggling shyly.

Tourist visitation to the Parc National des Volcans has changed the way of life here dramatically. Instead of indifference, the Rwandan attitude is now one of national pride toward the gorilla. It is a great hope for the survival of mountain gorillas.

* * *

In February of 1989, a year after my first visit to the gorillas, I returned to the Virunga Volcanoes, this time to Rwanda. Instead of a charter flight, I flew by commercial airline on a Boeing 737 Kenya Airways jet from Nairobi to Kigali, capital of Rwanda. There is, in fact, jet service three times weekly between the two cities. The flight, theoretically, takes two and one-half hours, though those who fly this route on a regular basis claim that the plane is considered on time if it arrives the same day it left. On this day my flight was only an hour late—certainly no worse than commercial airline service in the United States.

Rwanda is well prepared for an influx of tourism, judging by the new, modern airport. Equal-

ly impressive is the amount of new construction going on in Kigali. But my biggest surprise was the highway system—excellent by any standards and in contrast to the roads I had experienced in eastern Zaire. The road from Kigali to Gisenyi was built several years ago with the aid of the People's Republic of China. Paved and well maintained, this highway is better than some in Colorado. And nearly as scenic. Just outside Kigali, the highway climbs steeply in a series of serpentine curves, and when it levels out the road follows the crest of a ridge. The drive along this spine commands a spectacular view of the Nyabarongo River far below in a valley. The Nyabarongo and its tributaries are the source of the Nile; it flows into the Akagera River, which empties into Lake Victoria. Had Speke and Burton searched hard enough, they would have found that the Nile does not begin in Lake Victoria, but in the highlands of Rwanda nearly two hundred miles to the west. If they had followed it to its true source, they might have discovered, also, the mountain gorilla.

From here the road winds over verdant hills and down into lush valleys, past tea plantations, rice fields, groves of banana trees, coffee farms, and alongside rushing streams and through forests of tall, fragrant eucalyptus trees. The eucalyptus is not native. It was imported many years ago as a fast-growing substitute for the native forest, which had been cleared for agriculture. Groves of these tall trees are harvested peri-

Thatched-roof homes on the slopes of Mt. Karisimbi (in the background) on the way to visit the Suza Group.

odically for lumber and fuel. The countryside of Rwanda is perfumed by the wonderful redolence of burning eucalyptus.

On the drive from Kigali to Gisenyi, which takes about three hours, I noticed the cleanliness of the highway. There was practically no litter. In a poor country, there's little to waste, and cast-off items are often put to some use. Littering is a "luxury" found only in the over-developed countries.

As one approaches Ruhengeri, and when weather conditions allow, there's a view of the Virunga Volcanoes, spread in an arc roughly ten kilometers from town, to the north and northwest, rising grandly above the landscape: Karisimbi, Visoke, Sabinio, Gahinga, Muhabura, from left to right. From Ruhengeri, a road leads north to the park headquarters at Kinigi, the start for most of the visits to the gorillas.

We continued on the main highway, skirting the southern base of Mt. Karisimbi (which now has a television transmission tower on its summit!). As we came closer to Gisenyi, I could see flat-topped Nyarigongo Volcano to the west in Zaire. It looks as though someone had neatly sliced off the upper third of its pyramid-shaped cone and lifted it away for a look inside.

Gisenyi, on the northeast shore of Lake Kivu, has become a focal point for tourist visits to the mountain gorillas. Though it's an hour and one-half drive to Parc National des Volcans, the Meridien Hotel, in a lovely setting on the shore of the lake, is a first-class hotel by any standards in Africa. The town and surrounding area seem to have prospered from increased tourism. It's sad contrast to the squalid and depressing poverty of Goma only a few kilometers away in Zaire.

* * *

Seven others traveled with me on this trip: Wayne and Ginny King, some old friends who had formerly lived in Colorado; Ed and Sylvia Borg, friends from Florida; Emile Bernard; De-De Duchon; and Virginia Lyons. All are serious amateur photographers. None had been to Rwanda before. I was anxious to photograph the Rwandan gorillas, and, also, to observe firsthand the tourist operations here. After my visit to Zaire, I had a number of questions about long-term impact of tourism on gorillas.

There was a dim smudge of light in the eastern sky when we left the hotel at 6:00 A.M. and drove toward Ruhengeri. Because there were eight of us in our group, and because, at that time, there was a limit of six visitors to any gorilla family, we decided to split equally into two groups of four. The Kings and Emile and DeDe, in a separate vehicle, were to visit the Suza Group located high on the eastern flanks of Mt. Karisimbi. (The Suza Group had been named by Dian Fossey, many years ago, for the Suza River on the eastern slopes of Karisimbi; in a bit of puckish humor, she named the silverback John Philip. When Fossey first became aware of them, the family was small. But at the time of our visit, the Suza Group was the largest of any in the region, totaling thirty-three in all. The dominant silverback was named Imbaraga, and a younger silverback, Umugome, shared the leadership of the family.) The Borgs and Virginia and I were headed for Group 13, which normally ranges over the southwestern slopes of Mt. Sabinio. Our permits had been preassigned by the park service; we simply drew straws to see who would visit which group on which day.

The park headquarters at Kinigi is housed in a small brick building surrounded by gardens. Here, permits are checked, fees paid, and park rangers assigned to the people scheduled to visit any of the four gorilla families that have been habituated for tourism: Suza, Group 9, Group 11, and Group 13.

By the time all the paperwork was completed, it was 8:30. I was anxious to get underway, to take advantage of good early morning light for photography—and also to get to the gorillas before the usual late morning or early afternoon rainstorm hit. Before departing to the trailhead, we were met by Craig Sholley, director of Mountain Gorilla Project. MGP, funded by the African Wildlife Foundation, serves as advisor to the Rwandans for the tourism operation here, training and evaluating the park rangers and oth-

On the left is Mt. Mikeno, towering 14,553 feet, and on the right rises Mt. Karisimbi, 14,782 feet. This view is from the highway between Ginsenyi and Ruhengeri.

Imbaraga yawning. Those awesome canine teeth are used for breaking open vegetation such as bamboo. They are also used in fighting and can inflict mortal wounds. The black stains are from tartar buildup.

91

A visitor (left) and park ranger with Group 13. Park rules allow a total of only one hour of visitation per day to each gorilla family.

er personnel. Craig also oversees important antipoaching work in the park. The whole operation, he explained, is designed to achieve two goals: provide badly needed tourist income for Rwanda, and assure maximum protection for the mountain gorilla. Are the two goals compatible, I wondered aloud. If there's careful monitoring, Craig explained, there's no good reason why the two goals couldn't be attained. So far, things have gone reasonably well.

I reflected on two major problems that had been of concern to Dian Fossey and others in connection with tourist visitation to gorillas: disease transmission and increased stress on the animals. Mountain gorillas are susceptible to many viral and bacterial diseases that afflict humans; however, with no past exposure to some of these, the animals haven't built up natural immunity. Afflictions that may be minor for humans could be fatal to gorillas. Compounding the problem, much of the lower elevation of habitat of the gorillas has been lost to agricultural de-

velopment. The animals now live at higher, and thus colder and wetter, elevations, with the result that they may be more susceptible to respiratory infections. Especially with daily visitors, some of whom may be infected with cold viruses. Or worse.

Sholley admitted that this was difficult to monitor and control. The ranger-guides have been trained to be alert for people with obvious signs of colds such as coughing and sneezing and to deny them access. Also, visitors are asked to voluntarily step aside and not risk infecting the gorillas if they have an illness during the time of their visit. Some with illnesses had complied and given up their visit in the past, but I suspect that many, having spent thousands of dollars on a journey to Rwanda, would not willingly give up such an opportunity.

As illustration of the seriousness of the problem, in 1988 there was an outbreak of respiratory disease. Out of seven families monitored, six gorillas died. An autopsy on one of the animals

Hiking through bamboo forest on the way to Group 13 on the southwest slopes of Mt. Sabinio.

Mrithi, silverback of Group 13. The silvery color begins to appear in males at about age nine to ten. By twelve to thirteen years, adult males have prominent silvery coloring and are sexually mature and physically capable of leading a family. Females begin to reach sexual maturity when they are about seven and one-half years old.

Ndumi, silverback of Group 11.

indicated that it (not necessarily the others) had contracted measles! Its only possible cause was from human transmission. The ORTPN (Rwanda's department of tourism) approved a campaign for measles vaccination. The immunization was carried out by MGP and the Morris Animal Foundation veterinary clinic at Kinigi using low-pressure dart guns to inject vaccine. It was deemed successful, but not all gorillas could be vaccinated. And the very process itself causes added stress to the gorillas, which can hinder normal recovery of infected animals.

Sholley also was concerned about the gorillas' stress created by tourism. He felt that the present rule of allowing only six visitors to each family each day minimized strain on the animals. Also, in answer to my question about such late starts for trekking to the gorillas, he pointed out that this was beneficial. Visitation was timed so that people would arrive at a particular family near the middle of the day. This coincides with the normal relaxation time of gorillas, when they've had their morning feeding time and are taking a break. It's suggested that, being well fed and relaxed, the gorillas are less inclined to be stressed by visitors. My own observations seemed to bear that out, especially when I discovered some animals dozing off to sleep in our presence, totally unconcerned about us. However, like humans, there are individual temperaments and some are more nervous than others in the presence of people.

Our hike to Group 13 took about an hour and a half. The terrain was steep in places, and the sky threatened rain. Still, it was nice to be back in the Virunga rain forest. The greens seemed even more intense than I had remembered. The fragrances stirred memories of childhood days of those woodlands near home, with rich, earthy smells of damp foliage and decaying vegetation and the blends of sweetness and pungency from unknown plants. Despite aching muscles I was exhilarated. I understood clearly why Akeley and Schaller and Fossey had found this land so compelling. Perhaps somewhere in the hidden recesses of memory, at levels we are not aware of, maybe even gene-deep, there is this link with our primeval past. Being in the Virunga rain forest is like stepping back in time and seeing the world when it was young and fresh and savagely innocent.

We found Group 13 in thick forest on a steep hillside. Instead of resting, they were moving slowly through the brush and feeding. We followed at a respectful distance. The steepness and the vegetation made it difficult and I slipped frequently on wet foliage and mud. Finally Mrithi, the silverback, stopped in a patch of small plants to feed and other members of the group foraged slowly around us, feeding, playing. We were slightly uphill of Mrithi and he fed with his back to us. Occasionally he turned to give us a glance over his shoulder. Just checking, folks.

From our vantage point the hillside dropped steeply away and, looking over the brush, I was able to spot the park boundary. It seemed alarmingly close. The demarcation was dramatic: thick greenery of forest ended abruptly and beyond were the terraces and checkerboard patterns of farms. A sharp line separating two different worlds. Below me Mrithi and family munched away peacefully. I wondered if they ever looked out at those fields of civilization and pondered their significance. Had any ever ventured to the edge for a closer look? Did any of the older gorillas remember when those farmlands were forest, and did they recall the celery and nettles and *Galium* that were especially delectable? Mrithi wasn't saying.

Just before leaving, the vegetation to my right parted and a female moved slowly into view. She seemed plumper than the others, and I wondered if Mrithi's family was due for a new addition. Later I learned that the female, named Kwishima, gave birth about a month after my visit. The infant, a male, was named Kageli.

The next morning we repeated the long check-in procedure at Kinigi. This time, however, there were fewer of us. The trek to the Suza Group, an exhausting five-hour hike, had taken its toll. Three opted to stay at the hotel to rest tired muscles. We were down to five: the Kings, DeDe Duchon, Virginia Lyons, and I. Our destination was Group 11. Having nine gorillas, it was one

Ndumi and one of his youngsters. The silverbacks' affectionate, tender handling of their youngsters defied all the old myths I had heard about their savagery and ferociousness.

A juvenile climbs in a bunch of spindly bamboo, partly in play, and partly in search of tender young leaves to eat. Younger gorillas tend to be more agile climbers than their older patriarches and matriarches.

Boyd Norton photographing Ndumi, silverback leader of Group 11. (Photo © by Wayne and Ginny King)

of the smaller families.

Home ranges of mountain gorilla families are not permanently fixed, but for long periods the animals may lay claim to a particular area of forest over which they roam. The locale is determined by a number of factors, among them an abundance and variety of their food supply and the proximity of other gorilla families. Often there is some overlap of ranges and this may bring groups together and create conflict. Sometimes there is peaceful coexistence. In general, however, the family units try to isolate themselves from other families.

Group 11, led by the silverback Ndumi, roamed in the relatively flat saddle between Mt. Visoke and Mt. Sabinio, close to the northeast slopes of Visoke. Our hike was relatively easy, over gentle terrain that was flat. The trail meandered through lovely meadows, bordered by bamboo forests. We came across signs of buffalo, but they kept themselves well hidden in the forest. The ranger-guides carry rifles, ancient

weapons that probably saw service in World War I, as protection against buffalo. They claim they've never had to shoot any, which is reassuring, since in parts of East Africa there have been a number of fatalities from wild buffalo. Perhaps they are less aggressive here.

On a wooded hillside off the trail, a bushbuck stood silently, its reddish-brown hide contrasting sharply with the greenery. But in an instant it was gone, bounding off with a barking noise into deeper forest. Apparently the increased vigilance of antipoaching patrols has kept these forest antelope from being exterminated.

Two hours of hiking brought us close to the Zaire border. The land ahead sloped away and we looked out on a vast expanse of dense forest from a vantage point above the forest canopy. The distant line of trees snared and entangled the vaporous clouds of mist. Somewhere ahead, as near as I could determine, was the area where I had visited Rugabo and family the previous year.

Ndumi was napping as we approached. We

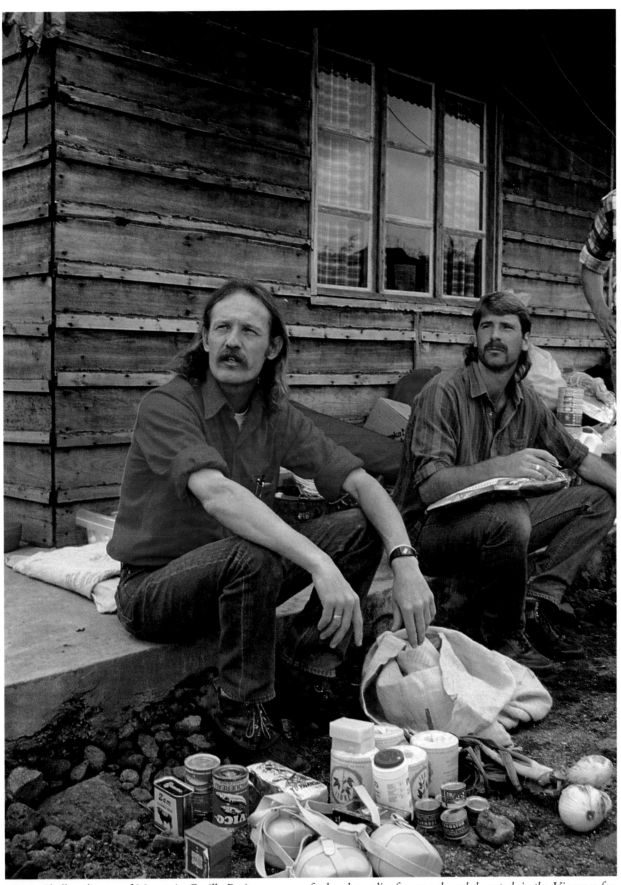

Craig Sholley, director of Mountain Gorilla Project, prepares food and supplies for several-week-long trek in the Virungas for a gorilla census in September 1989. Results of census indicated an increase of about 10 percent in mountain gorilla population for Rwanda, Zaire, and Uganda. Total number of mountain gorillas is at least 310, up from 279 in 1986.

walked as noiselessly as possible, the guides leading the way and softly vocalizing "*mahem, mahem*" to reassure the gorillas that we were friends. The big silverback, about fifteen feet away and sprawled on some matted-down foliage, opened his eyes and yawned, displaying an imposing set of canine teeth. As cameras and motor drives clicked and whirred, Ndumi yawned again, picked his teeth, scratched himself, then closed his eyes to nap again. One of the guides took a newspaper out of his pack, leaned against a tree, and perused the local news! Just another quiet day in the Virungas.

Hunger finally stirred Ndumi from his snooze. He sat up and moved into the brush. A short distance away, he sat down to feed. As I raised the camera for a picture I noticed for the first time that his right hand was missing. Where the hand should have been was a healed-over and well-calloused stump. Apparently as a youngster, Ndumi had tangled with a poacher's wire snare. He had been lucky that he hadn't died of infection, as so many other gorillas had. Even though he survived, the accident undoubtedly caused great and prolonged suffering.

Group 11 seems to have had more than its share of entanglement with snares: Kosa, a twelve-year-old blackback male, had lost most of his arm; Mikeno, another silverback that had been with the group for a while, also was missing a hand.

Ndumi plucked leaves with delicate grace using his good hand and placed them in his mouth. His infirmity in no way detracted from his dignity. Yet I had this overwhelming sadness, mixed with anger. "Look here, Ndumi," I wanted to say, "maybe all this pain and suffering caused by my species is finally coming to an end. Maybe now your children will be safe from this sort of thing." Maybe. Ndumi munched away, casting an occasional glance in our direction. He seemed to hold no grudge.

I walked in silence for most of the way back.

* * *

September 1989, my third trip. The young-

sters alongside the road stared, wide-eyed, at a silver-haired stranger driving by in a four-wheel-drive Suzuki. Their looks were curious, perhaps incredulous, but not malevolent; occasionally some waved and I waved back.

It takes about a half hour to drive from the Hotel Muhabura in Ruhengeri to the headquarters for Parc National des Volcans in Kinigi. Just as I turned onto the road to Kinigi, I stopped to pick up a young man hitchhiking (instead of the thumb out gesture, the hitchhikers here, as in most of Africa, hold their hand out, palm down, sometimes with a slight wave of the hand). I guessed his age at about twenty, and I tried to engage him in conversation. His English was about as good as my French, meaning that it was bad, and my Swahili, in which most Rwandans are fluent, is barely adequate for conversation. And so, half in English and half in Swahili, I learned that he is a guide, working for the national park. I asked about the gorillas—trying to measure the attitudes of people here about these animals. It was difficult to converse, but along that bumpy road I slowly gathered this impression: He was fiercely proud of the mountain gorilla, of the efforts to protect the species and of the work done to stop poaching. I gathered, also, that his job is a prestigious one, the envy, apparently, of his peers. It wasn't easy to learn all this because the conversation was one in which each of us, groping for correct words and phrases, spoke haltingly in monosyllables. It was like two children conversing for the first time. We baby-talked our way to Kinigi.

We exchanged au revoirs at the park headquarters, then I continued on the road to the east a few hundred yards more, to the turnoff to Craig Sholley's home.

The house was in the center of a fenced yard and commanded a fine view of Mts. Sabinio, Gahinga, and Muhabura. Pale, bell-shaped blossoms of *Datura stramonium* drooped over one of the fences, an exotic plant probably imported from North America decades ago and now growing wild in many parts of Africa. In the center of the backyard was a planter brimming with the white, daisylike flowers of pyrethrum and in

Adult mountain gorillas, the silverback included, seem very tolerant of the energetic and often mischievous behavior of youngsters. Discipline is rarely physical. Instead, stern vocalizations in the form of piglike grunts or emphatic body posturing or strong looks serve to reprimand a rowdy youngster.

the center of this patch was a small banana tree. Mt. Sabinio loomed above, its outline ghostly in early morning mist and cloud.

I found Craig outside his house, sitting in the midst of what looked like the aftermath of an explosion in a grocery store. Strewn about were cans of powdered milk and tuna fish and corned beef, bags of rice and beans, boxes of matches, rolls of toilet paper, lanterns and flashlights, detergent, water jugs and canteens, tea and coffee. Craig and his assistants were preparing for a long trek in the Virungas.

The Mountain Gorilla Project was about to undertake the largest and, they hoped, the most accurate census of mountain gorillas ever conducted. Teams of workers would spend the next four to five weeks ranging over most of the protected gorilla habitat in Rwanda, Zaire, and Uganda. Backpacking through the miles of unbroken rain forest would allow them to make contact with unhabituated and rarely seen gorilla families. Even where direct contact wasn't made,

reasonably accurate figures would be obtained by tracking families and counting night nests and dung deposits. The last census had been done in 1986 and indicated a minimum population of 279 gorillas. That was an increase of forty gorillas over the 1981 count. Craig was optimistic that this new one would indicate another increase in population.

Craig Sholley has lived in Africa, off and on, for the past eighteen years. His involvement began in 1973 as a Peace Corps worker in the town of Bukavu, south of Lake Kivu and not far from Rwanda. He had obtained a bachelor's degree in biology and a master's in administration. His assignment was to develop school science programs for the government in Zaire.

In 1978, Craig came to Rwanda under a grant from Louis Leakey and spent thirteen months working for Dian Fossey at the Karisoke Research Center. Later, he led occasional natural history tours to parts of East Africa. In 1987, the African Wildlife Foundation asked him to as-

Mt. Mikeno, 14,553 feet, seen from the highway between Gisenyi and Ruhengeri.

sume directorship of the Mountain Gorilla Project.

Craig had been under some recent stress. Between the time of my visit in February and my return in September, the ORTPN had unilaterally decided to increase the number of visitors each day to the gorilla families from six to eight. The reason: to boost the income to the government from tourism. Craig was against it, arguing that increasing the number of visitors made it harder for the guides to control the people and to maintain strict adherence to park rules. And most importantly, it would increase the risk of transmitting human-borne infections.

During some of my previous visits to the gorillas, there had been fewer visitors than the six-people limit. But more and more people were coming here, perhaps out of fear that the mountain gorillas will soon become extinct. Many have been attracted by the movie *Gorillas in the Mist*.

Undoubtedly, tourism has contributed greatly to saving the mountain gorilla. In 1988, gorilla tourism was second only to coffee and tea export for foreign currency income in Rwanda. It may well be first very soon. The Rwandan government recognizes the important economic value and, according to some, the mountain gorilla now may be the best protected animal in Africa. Craig Sholley credits this to what he termed biodiplomacy, the long-term cooperation devoted to preserving the mountain gorillas that he and the Karisoke researchers established with the Rwandan government.

The future is not at all certain. The population of mountain gorillas is still precarious. An outbreak of a serious infectious disease could have grave impact on the population. Some worry about the viability of the gene pool and possible inbreeding that may weaken the species.

Will there be mountain gorillas one hundred years from now? Craig Sholley answered: "Who knows? Will there be *people* a hundred years from now? I can only say that I'm cautiously optimistic. The outlook is certainly more positive now than it was, say, ten years ago. If our current census shows more growth in the gorilla population,

there's reason for more optimism."

* * *

When we left the vehicle, the summit of Mt. Karisimbi was clear against a backdrop of bright blue sky. The morning air was crisp and lucid. We hiked up the steep trail past terraces of corn and wheat and potatoes, past thatched-roof *bandas* flanked with red-blossomed flame trees. Soon we were high enough to look out over the valley to the east and south. The land undulated gently, rising up to some distant, soft green hills. The lovely patchwork patterns of farms were bright green against the red-brown volcanic soil, again making me think of Tolkien.

It took us almost five hours of hiking and a climb of three thousand feet to reach the park boundary. From there we entered some very dense *Hagenia* forest, following a narrow, slippery trail. The weather, as usual, had deteriorated. Rain began to fall, lightly at first, then heavier as we moved deeper into the forest. Fortunately we did not have to go far to find the Suza Group.

Imbaraga was sitting, Buddha-like, under a gnarled *Hagenia* tree. Rain poured down. The silverback had his arms folded across his chest, looking like a stern schoolmaster. A few feet to his left, a youngster played in the midst of a tangle of vines, stopping frequently to snatch some leafy morsel and pop it into its mouth. To the right of Imbaraga, one of the females snuggled up close to him, laying her head against his massive body. Raindrops glistened on their dark, furry coats. I felt like an intruder, but the three of them sat and watched us impassively. Is it possible, I wondered, that we have become a form of entertainment for them?

The rain stopped, but the forest still dripped. Imbaraga unfolded his arms and walked four-legged to the left, placing each knuckle firmly on the forest floor. He was enormous; every movement conveyed a sense of power. Across his shoulders he must have measured close to four feet. His upper arms were larger than my thighs. Yet there was a sense of grace and gentleness in his demeanor. He moved about ten feet, under another spreading branch of the same tree, and sprawled out on his side. He laid his head down on his crooked arm. The female had followed and lay next to him, her head on his side.

One of the guides had led the rest of our group to visit other members of the family several yards away, but I lingered behind with the other guide. I wanted a few more photographs of Imbaraga, but mostly I just wanted to sit quietly and watch for a few more moments. The great silverback lifted his head and yawned a huge, cavernous yawn, then looked at me. Again I felt that strange chill, a sense of some unspoken communication. I smiled. He yawned again. We watched each other. Then he laid his head down and closed his eyes.

Too soon our visit was up. We walked back through the wet forest and I glanced back to see if I could spot any of the gorillas, and especially Imbaraga. They were hidden by the dense foliage.

As we began our hike down the steep hillside, a storm engulfed Mt. Sabinio to the northeast. Curtains of rain swept toward us. Lightning flashed in the dark sky. Thunder rumbled across the valley. Looking back once more, I saw the forest disappear in mist. And I was on my way home.

A juvenile, between two and three years of age, and a member of the Suza family.

The People of Rwanda. *Rwandans are warm and friendly. And in recent years, the mountain gorillas have become a source of pride to the people.*

The People of Rwanda. *Rwanda is a lovely country, aside from the fascinating gorillas and the beauty of the Virunga Volcanoes.*

The People of Rwanda. *Life is tough here. Farming is still done largely by hand; lumber is cut by hand in sawpits. The colorful marketplaces are gatherings for selling produce and items such as baskets and pots.*

The People of Rwanda. *Perhaps the greatest threat to the mountain gorilla is population pressure. Rwanda is the most densely populated country in Africa. The need for food results in most available land being used for crop cultivation. Even the steepest mountainsides are cleared of forest, terraced, and planted. In both Rwanda and Zaire, land clearing and cultivation take place right to the very edge of the national parks.*

The People of Rwanda. *Curiously enough, it is people pressure of another kind—tourism—that may save the gorillas. Increasing numbers of people come to the parks in Rwanda and Zaire to visit and photograph these gentle creatures. Using methods pioneered by Dian Fossey, park rangers have habituated certain gorilla families to the presence of small groups of people on a regular basis.*

111

The People of Rwanda. *The economic boost from tourism has provided strong incentives for both the Rwandan and Zairoise governments to control poaching and protect the gorillas and their habitat. Strict controls are placed on visitation, and monitoring the impact of tourism is carefully carried out by a number of organizations. Despite—or perhaps because of—such limitations, tourism to the gorilla parks has been flourishing. Reservations are booked for many months—even up to a year—in advance.*

The People of Rwanda. *In the past, large acreages were given over to growing pyrethrum, used as a natural insecticide. But the market has diminished in recent years. Tourism to Volcanoes National Park is now the largest source of foreign income and provides incentive for the Rwandans to ensure protection of the gorillas.*

The People of Rwanda. *Will it work? Can tourists and gorillas and Rwandans coexist? Are there any long-term impacts that tourism might have on the mountain gorillas (such as disease or behavioral modification)? Tough questions. There aren't any quick answers.*

EPILOGUE

Things have changed since my first and last visits to the gorillas. What effects these changes will have, only time will tell.

The fate of the Djomba Intrepids Camp in Zaire is uncertain. United Touring Company, a major international travel company and one of the partners in the camp, has dissolved its relationship with the Zairoise partner and stopped sending visitors there. The last camp manager quit. No one seems to know if it is open for business anymore.

The result of the Mountain Gorilla Project September 1989 census indicated a minimum of 310 gorillas in the Virungas, an increase of thirty-one gorillas over the 1986 survey, and representing a growth in population of more than 10 percent.

Craig Sholley is no longer director of the Mountain Gorilla Project. In early 1990, all control and direction was assumed by the Rwandan government, with the aid and cooperation of the African Wildlife Foundation. Craig remains an advisor to the African Wildlife Foundation.

The number of visitors to some of the gorilla families was dropped back to six people per day; specifically, Group 9 and Group 11 will have only six visitors. Group 13 and the Suza Group, however, will continue to have eight visitors per day.

The Karisoke Research Center still conducts important research and remains under the auspices of the Digit Fund. The new director of Karisoke is Diane Doran, an experienced researcher whose studies include behavior of the pygmy chimpanzee in Zaire.

* * *

Imbaraga, the splendid and gentle silverback of the Suza Group, died on April 8, 1990. He was estimated to be about thirty years old—not especially old for silverbacks. An autopsy revealed the cause of death to be pneumonia. Twenty of the group's thirty-three members had severe respiratory problems but were expected to recover. It was reported that, as he lay dying, the members of his family came to Imbaraga and touched him or lay with him or otherwise said goodbye to their leader.

Imbaraga, silverback leader of the Suza Group, relaxing under a Hagenia tree during a rainstorm. This photo was made about seven months before his death from pneumonia.

VISITING THE MOUNTAIN GORILLAS

GETTING THERE

Under ideal conditions it's possible to step aboard a jet in New York on a Sunday evening and by Tuesday morning be sitting next to a gorilla family in the heart of Volcanoes National Park in Rwanda. Tourist excursions to Rwanda have increased dramatically in recent years. However, don't expect to visit the Karisoke Research Center. Access to Karisoke is very tightly controlled and limited only to certain select and bona fide researchers and occasional journalists. Instead, there are four gorilla families, separate from Karisoke, to which tourists are allowed to pay a visit — and under very tightly controlled conditions.

Most visits to the mountain gorillas are done as an add-on to an East African safari, so if you have such a trip planned you might ask your tour operator about an extension to Rwanda. If you're just thinking about an African trip, I recommend Voyagers International (addresses for all companies are below) as a safari outfitter and for arranging your trip to Rwanda. I've used Voyagers exclusively for my overseas photography workshops, and there's none better.

For do-it-yourselfers, Rwanda is served by Sabena Airlines, Air France and, from Nairobi, Kenya Airways. You'll need to obtain permits to visit the gorillas. (A prime advantage to using a safari outfitter is that all this will be taken care of for you.) Be sure to apply for permits at least four months in advance. If you plan to be in Nairobi and want to make arrangements there, East Africa Ornithological Safaris can secure permits and provide for all your lodging and travel. Rwanda Travel Service in Kigali is able to secure gorilla permits, make hotel reservations, and provide driver-guides. Also, they can provide you with a rental vehicle, should you choose to go it alone.

AND ONCE YOU'RE THERE

As visitors to the mountain gorillas we all must assume the role of steward. Take care not to leave anything in the forest; if anything is dropped, pick it up. Gorillas may come by and find the litter; it could transmit disease. Follow the regulations of the park and adhere to the directives of the park guides. Most importantly, never make physical contact with a gorilla or allow one to touch you (youngsters, in particular, are curious and will often approach closely). The guides will prevent contact, but at times they may be distracted and not notice one approaching. Above all, forego your visit it you have any infectious disease! Even a common cold could cause serious, if not fatal, problems in a gorilla family.

Voyagers International
P.O. Box 915
Ithaca, NY 14851
Tel: (607) 257-3091
FAX: (607) 257-3699

East Africa Ornithological Safaris
P.O. Box 48019
Nairobi, Kenya
Tel: 331684
FAX: 725316

Rwanda Travel Service
43 Bd de la Revolution
B.P. 140 Kigali, Rwanda
Tel: 72210

Pushing our way through giant nettles on a trail cut by the pangas *of our ranger guides. We were on the way to Group 11 near the Zaire border.*

NOTES ON
THE PHOTOGRAPHY

Mountain gorillas have been some of the toughest subjects I've ever had to photograph. Not because they weren't cooperative—they were—but because of the frequent dim lighting, rain and mist, dense forest, and often difficult terrain.

Most of the photographs in this book were made with Leica cameras and a couple of older model, nonelectronic Nikons. I chose the Leicas because they are so rugged and hold up well under the tough conditions found in the Virungas. The modern, all-electronic, autofocusing cameras don't seem to function well in the cold, soggy environment here. I've seen a few of them die just when we found ourselves in excellent position to photograph gorillas.

Dim lighting in the forests dictates use of fast films and fast lenses. (Incidentally, park rules prohibit use of flash, a wise edict because it helps minimize impact of human visitation on the gorillas.) The best all-around film choice, in my opinion, is Kodachrome 200. It has superb color and sharpness, considering its speed. I usually rate the speed at 300 because I think it's a little faster than Kodak claims. For times when the lighting is *really* bad, I carry a number of rolls of 800/1600 Ektachrome; I don't like to use these faster films unless I really have to because they are very grainy.

Lenses. I shot many of these pictures with Leica 70–210 and 35–70 zoom lenses. The problem with zooms is that they are slow, with a maximum aperture of only f/3.5 or f/4. I found a 180mm f/2.8 lens and an 80mm f/1.4 lens to be very useful at times. Lenses longer than 200mm aren't of much use here; the forest is too thick for long distance shots and besides, often you are as close as fifteen or twenty feet from the gorillas.

A female carries her six-month-old youngster on her back. Rugabo family, Virunga National Park (Parc National de Virunga), Zaire.

HOW YOU CAN HELP
THE MOUNTAIN GORILLA

Continued research and constant vigilance are still required to assure the survival of the mountain gorilla. Your financial support of these organizations will help them carry out these tasks:

African Wildlife Foundation
1717 Massachusetts Avenue N.W.
Washington, D.C. 20036

The Digit Fund
P.O. Box 308
Bristol
BS99 7LQ

Karisoke Research Center
The Digit Fund
45 Inverness Drive East
Englewood, CO 80112-5480

The Flora and Fauna Preservation
  Society
79–83 North Street
Brighton
East Sussex
BN1 1ZA

The International Primate Protection
  League
19–25 Argyll Street
London
W1V 2DU

The Primate Society of Great Britain
Department of Psychology
University of Reading
White Knights
Reading
Berkshire

World Wide Fund for Nature U.K.
Panda House
Weyside Park
Godalming
Surrey
GU7 1XR

REFERENCES

Akeley, Carl E. *In Brightest Africa*, New York: Garden City, 1923.

Akeley, Mary L. Jobe. *Carl Akeley's Africa*, New York: Dodd, Mead & Co., 1930.

Akeley, Mary L. Jobe. *Congo Eden*, New York: Dodd, Mead & Co., 1950.

Barns, T. Alexander. *Across the Great Craterland to the Congo*, New York: Knopf, 1924.

Bradley, Mary Hastings. *On the Gorilla Trail*, New York: D. Appleton & Co., 1922.

Dixson, A. *The Natural History of the Gorilla*, London: Weidenfeld and Nicolson, 1981.

Du Chaillu, Paul. *Explorations and Adventures in Equatorial Africa*, New York: Harper & Bros., 1861.

Du Chaillu, Paul. *Stories of Gorilla Country*, New York: Harper & Bros., 1868.

Fossey, Dian. *Gorillas in the Mist*, Boston: Houghton Mifflin, 1983.

Fossey, Dian. "Making Friends with Mountain Gorillas." *National Geographic* 137 (1970): 48–67.

Fossey, Dian. "More Years with Mountain Gorillas." *National Geographic* 140 (1971): 574–585.

Fossey, Dian. "The Imperiled Mountain Gorilla." *National Geographic* 159 (1981): 501–523.

Goodall, Alan. *The Wandering Gorillas*, London: Collins, 1979.

Gregory, William K., and Henry C. Raven. *In Quest of Gorillas*, New Bedford, MA: Darwin Press, 1937.

Mowat, Farley. *Woman in the Mists*, New York: Warner Books, 1988.

Merfield, Fred G., and Harry Miller. *Gorilla Hunter*, New York: Farrar, Straus & Cudahy, 1937.

Schaller, George B. *The Year of the Gorilla*, Chicago: University of Chicago Press, 1961.

Schaller, George B. *The Mountain Gorilla: Ecology and Behavior*, Chicago: University of Chicago Press, 1963.

Speke, John Hanning. *Journey of the Discovery of the Source of the Nile*. New York: Harper & Bros., 1868.

Stanley, Henry M. *How I Found Livingstone*. New York: Charles Scribner's Sons, 1906.

Zahl, Paul A. "Face to Face with Gorillas in Central Africa." *National Geographic* 117 (1960): 114–137.

Overleaf: An adult female from Group 13 peers out from ferns and foliage.